SASS: Fifty Years of

Social Work Education

SASS: Fifty Years

of Social Work

Education

A HISTORY OF THE SCHOOL

OF APPLIED SOCIAL SCIENCES,

CASE WESTERN RESERVE UNIVERSITY

by Thomas F. Campbell

THE PRESS OF

CASE WESTERN RESERVE UNIVERSITY

1967

This book was written and put into production
before the federation of Western Reserve University
and Case Institute of Technology, in July, 1967.
The name of the new institution, of which the School
of Applied Social Sciences is a part, is Case Western
Reserve University.

Printed in the United States of America by the Oberlin Printing
Company, Oberlin, Ohio.

Library of Congress Catalogue Card Number 66-28141.

Contents

Contents

Illustrations

Introduction

The history of the development of human vocations and of the development of some of them into professions exhibits a great consistency. As should be expected, the history of the development of the learning process for the vocations and of the training and educational process for the professions exhibits a similar consistency.

All human arts have begun on a pragmatic basis of trial and error. As experience has shown that some actions produce desirable consequences while others have had less success, a body of practice has developed and a vocation been established, the members of which have been recognized as skilled practitioners. In some vocations human curiosity has been directed toward the body of experience in an attempt to understand, to rationalize, and particularly to improve their practice. The fruits of such curiosity have led in two directions. The first is to produce concepts which have led to generalizations and the formulation of principles. The second is to produce or to identify abstract knowledge which is relevant to the practice of the vocation. Both of these results produce changes in the practice and a vocation begins to exhibit the characteristic of a profession. The particular practice requires both skill and knowledge and the relation between these two produces a mutual force for growth and for change. At first, the growth is slow and change almost imperceptible. But the effect of a mutuality is one of acceleration, and growth quickens and change becomes clearly evident.

During the period that any art is based purely on pragmatic experience, the preparation of the young for being its future practitioners is in learning by doing. The mechanism for the learning process is the apprenticeship. The objective of the learning process is the transference, over a relatively long period of time, of all the skill and experience of the master to the neophyte. When conceptualization appears, a part of the training process becomes the oral or written transmission of these concepts and the principles which derive from them. At this point the process of preparation begins to show some of the characteristics of education.

Frequently the profession begins to organize simple schools for the training of its future members. The teachers are practitioners who both instruct and serve as master practitioners demonstrating their skills. This phase may be of short or long duration depending upon the rate of change that occurs in response to internal or external forces. It is characterized by control by the guild or the profession. As this system of training becomes insufficient or unsatisfactory, consideration is given to sharing responsibility and control with some part of the formal educational structure.

It is at this point of development that professional education has entered the university. Initially, it has been little more than a partial transfer of responsibility. The faculty is at first constituted of successful practitioners, and the instructional method is still largely of an apprenticeship nature. Little scholarly effort is expected or permitted on the part of the teachers, and no formal research is provided for.

However, the new professional school does not long remain impervious to its university environment. The relevance of the knowledge of the university disciplines becomes evident. The beneficial effect of research is seen, and the relationship of knowledge to skill appears more obvious. Teachers become interested in their own further development and follow a program of study to broaden their knowledge and to share interests with scholars in pertinent fields. The learning process broadens and matures, and formal education replaces apprenticeship training. It is at this point that a practicing art moves to become a learned profession, and the professional begins to become a bivalent person—both a knower and a doer.

In some vocations the evolution requires a very long time for accomplishment. In some, the evolution never occurs. In the vocation of social work the period of evolution has been surprisingly brief. The history of the first fifty years of the School of Applied Social Sciences of Western Reserve University attests to this.

—John S. Millis

Foreword

The history of any professional school reflects during its lifetime the development of the profession of which it is a part, as well as the history of education for the profession. The beginnings at the turn of the century of formal social work education stemmed from the pre-eminent leadership of Mary Richmond. The objective of such education was to prepare social workers more systematically for the responsibilities they would eventually carry, mainly in voluntary social agencies. This involved work with individuals and families, so that social casework was a primary focus.

While many schools, such as the School of Applied Social Sciences, began partly with the objective of improvement of social welfare on a general scale, and included content in economic and social reform in their programs, this was not the central thrust of social work education in the 1920's and 1930's, by which time most schools of social work in the United States were organized. There was, however, an increasing relationship to the requirements of daily practice in social work and the application of academic studies to the pursuit of more effective social work practice. Great attention was placed on field instruction in co-operating social agencies. Disciplined supervision in field work and the effort to use the field experience to translate academic study into the needs and realities of practice continued to present vital features of social work education. At the same time, there was an undercurrent of apprenticeship ideology in this training, particularly in the early decades.

From the 1920's to the 1940's social work shifted from "cause"—emphasis on social movement—to "function"—emphasis on method—to use the terms coined by Porter Lee in 1929. It was not until the 1950's that a return to more balance between social objectives and professional methodology began.

Most schools of social work began either within, or in association with, universities. After a long period of relative estrangement from the academic climate and system of the university—an estrangement which sometimes threatened the very existence of schools and adversely affected their academic standards—they have moved closer to their university bases. Strains consequently occurred in their relationships to the social agencies with which they had been so intimately and principally identified. With the growth, particularly during the 1950's and 1960's, of emphasis on higher academic credentials among faculty, with the return to more potent relationships with the social and behavioral sciences and the growth of doctoral programs, schools of social work have increasingly acquired a stronger university perspective. While the relationship to community agencies has remained very close and essential, the sphere of educational jurisdiction is no longer intimately shared.

Among the issues involved in the place of the school of social work in the university has been the school's relationship to research and to service as well as to teaching. These functions reflect those of the university as a whole. Schools of social work, however, have been far more oriented toward service than have been most other components of the university, particularly in the private university. Questions of appropriateness in the areas of research and service are, therefore, particularly keen for schools of social work. In the production of scientific research the boundaries of what is relevant are as yet often ambiguous in contrast, for example, to research stemming from academic departments in the social and behavioral sciences.

The interpretation of what constitutes legitimate service by the school beyond its educational function has broadened. For many years such service consisted primarily in providing special training for agencies outside of the school's own professional program, in providing consultation and other efforts to use a training function more broadly. The conception of service has now widened to include initiating and demonstrating new modes of social work practice in communities and, indeed, attempting both to study and to make a direct impact on social welfare policy.

In 1915 Abraham Flexner noted several attributes of social work

2  1967

DT
714
.N3516
1986

Namibia in the 1980s. -- 2nd ed. --
London : Catholic Institute for
International Relations and the
British Council of Churches, 1986.
83 p. : ill. ; 21 cm. -- (A Future
for Namibia ; 1)
Previous ed. published also in
series: A CIIR/BCC position paper
Bibliography: p. 67.
ISBN 0-946848-44-0 (pbk.)

that could make it a profession. He raised doubts, however, about whether it was a distinct field or simply served other professions, and had questions about its organizational attributes. Since that time, social work has met the specifications he noted. It has formed a strong and large professional organization, developed a code of ethics, and published a number of journals; and its professional schools have formed a Council on Social Work Education with accrediting authority. While the boundaries of social work have never been altogether defined, it is increasingly recognized as a profession, based in knowledge, with a high sense of responsibility and a socially sanctioned set of functions.

Today, at a period in which there is the greatest support for social work education, the greatest demand for professionally educated social workers, the highest level of interest in undergraduate social work education, and the most favorable climate within universities, there is less complacency than ever in social work education.

The central issues are identifiable. One of the major problems has been the need to develop a conceptual context for social work practice. The boundaries of what constitutes "professional social work" have become wider and wider and the edges less defined. Professional social work education has taken the route that education in other professions has taken, namely, to broaden the base of professional education and so to assume that specializations could follow after this period. The long-range trend has been to try to teach a core of fundamentals while preparing students for practice in casework, group work, or community organization.

This trend is now seriously questioned. The predominant school of thought continues to hold that the retention of these divisions is essential, both to study and develop these methods of practice properly and to enable social work graduates to enter the field of social work as more responsible practitioners. Another presses, however, for even more fundamental preparation in generalized "social work practice" for students who will be going into all areas of social work. Still another advocates, through a differentiated curriculum, the preparation of at least two kinds of social workers, those who will be going into fields of direct practice with individuals and groups and those who will be entering into fields of social planning and administration.

Another issue concerns the relationship of professional education to other social work training. With most individuals engaged in social work occupations having no graduate professional education, the question arises whether graduate social work education should be linked in any way with undergraduate pre-social work programs, particularly in the light of a severe social work manpower shortage. In ways similar to developments in other professions, social work has recognized the importance of differentiating responsibilities along the lines of different levels of educational preparation. It has also recognized the desirability of changing the patterns, in both the organization and the practice of social work, to make more effective utilization of appropriate education and experience.

The history of the School of Applied Social Sciences of Western Reserve University has reflected these general trends and is absorbed in both definition and resolution of the current issues. Because of the contributions made by all those associated with it during its first fifty years, the capacity of the School to face the promise and the uncertainties of social work education in the future has never been stronger.

—Herman D. Stein

Preface

This short history of the School of Applied Social Sciences is based primarily upon the School's records: minutes, memorandums, correspondence, and the annual reports of the deans—to which the School and the University gave me unrestricted access. Footnotes have been kept to a minimum.

I am indebted to Dean Herman D. Stein and the following faculty members for their willingness to take time to talk about the School: Arthur Blum, Raymond Fisher, Margaret Hartford, Margaret Johnson, Arden Melzer, Willard Richan, Irving Rosow, John B. Turner, and Ruth Werner. The librarian of SASS, Mrs. Martha Stewart; the university archivist, Mrs. Ruth Helmuth; the dean's secretary, Mrs. Joyce S. Wightman; and the School's registrar, Miss Margaret Hopkins, were always willing to answer questions and assist me in locating material.

The staff of the Press of Western Reserve University provided advice and encouragement when both were needed. Dean Carl F. Wittke, Miss Carolyn Neff, James B. Gidney, and Edwin P. Marcus read the manuscript and offered valuable suggestions. Finally, I acknowledge the great debt I owe my wife, Marguerite Brown Campbell (SASS, 1956), in the writing of this history.

T.F.C.
August 16, 1966

SASS: Fifty Years of

Social Work Education

I.

Prelude to a Profession:
The Local Scene

When the pioneers slowly infiltrated into the virgin lands of the Connecticut Western Reserve at the close of the eighteenth century, their way of life was as simple and uncluttered as their belongings were few in number. In the territory along the shores of Lake Erie which was to become metropolitan Cleveland, frontier conditions determined the social structure of men's lives. If illness, death, or other disaster struck a family, a simple concept of charity prevailed. Friends gathered to harvest the crops, care for the stricken, and offer solace to their neighbors in trouble.

But as the land was settled and villages and towns began to develop, this primitive egalitarianism began to disappear. The community sought to protect itself from the intrusion of the pauper through a systematized governmental structure that was a derivative of the English Poor Law of 1601. Responsibility for the poor was placed on the local government, but the principle of requiring that those given aid must have lived in the community for at least one year became increasingly obsolete in the mobile American society. By 1836, the year the city of Cleveland was incorporated by the state of Ohio, township records contained many references to warrants directing the Overseer of the Poor to order paupers to leave town—so that they did not become a burden on the local citizenry.

The problem of the poor who did not meet the year's residence requirement was aggravated by the growth of the city's commercial activities on the Ohio Canal and the Great Lakes. When these waterways were frozen during the winter months, sailors and longshoremen were unemployed, until the warm days of spring melted the ice. It was this condition of seasonal unemployment that led to the creation of the Cleveland chapter of the American Seamen's Friend Society in 1830. The organization's principal objective was to preach the gospel, but it also provided temporary relief for seamen, dockworkers, and their families. Because the Society clearly stated its intention of serving those "otherwise unreached by denominational agencies," it became the first Cleveland charity to receive donations from the public at large.[1]

Although organizations with religious affiliation were numerous throughout the nineteenth century, the concept of assisting the worthy poor regardless of religious affiliation became increasingly important during the growth of urbanized society. After the Civil War the inrush of immigrants from a multitude of European countries destroyed the social and religious homogeneity of the community. The rapid industrialization of the city brought problems too massive to be handled by small religious and ethnic groups, which had supplemented the meager public assistance in the past. Traditional roles of support within the family unit were weakened or destroyed in the move from the farm to the city—particularly when the move was to a strange land. The ugly aspects of urbanization, such as inadequate housing, disease, and the devastating effect of unemployment caused by recurrent contractions of the business cycle, demanded a less sectarian approach to relief of poverty.

Furthermore, tax-supported relief was viewed with increasing suspicion by the Protestant middle class, which saw its community inundated by "foreigners." The inadequate principles of the old English poor law were never revised to allow the local government to meet realistically the needs of urban society. Philip Klein of the New York School of Social Work has perceptively characterized the philosophy of nineteenth-century charity: ". . . The status of poor relief and its philosophical substructure were essentially what they had been for three centuries. [The community] assumed that poverty was the effect of shiftlessness and irresponsible character weakness rather than of external circumstances."[2]

The periodic reorganizations of the successors to the Seamen's Friend Society during the nineteenth century illustrate the community's changing attitude toward the function of private charity and its administration. In 1867 the Society became the Cleveland Bethel Union and began to form patterns of activity that ultimately made it the most influential private charity organization in

Cleveland. Although the Union continued to send reports to the parent body of the American Seamen's Friend Society, a group of leading Cleveland businessmen and their wives became trustees, charged with complete responsibility for "the thorough business management" of the agency. While the missionary functions of the Union were retained, the organization broadened its scope to include not only seamen but also "the neglected in the lower part of the city." Volunteers, working through the Ladies Bethel and Mission Aid Society, visited immigrant families. The nineteenth-century charity program of friendly visiting was based on the premise that the moral exhortations of volunteers could inculcate middle-class standards of temperance, sanitation, frugality, and hard work; but the program also served to make many visitors acutely aware of the pressing problems of "strangers in a strange land."

Between 1860 and 1870 Cleveland more than doubled its population. The economic distress of the newcomers that resulted from the Panic of 1873 gave impetus to the further expansion of the Union, which created the Bethel Relief Association in that year. Recognizing the fact that the Union's work had become "nearly general," the reorganized Association expanded its relief work "to furnish temporary aid and employment as far as practicable, to the worthy poor of the city . . . not otherwise provided for—rendering assistance to such as are willing to help themselves, so far as they are able, but who from sickness, want of work and other misfortunes are for a time in need of aid."[3] Despite such recognition of the environmental causes of poverty, the community continued to fear that giving relief destroyed the moral fiber of recipients unless it was "earned" by hard work. The Association not only operated an active employment bureau but also provided a wood-yard for hard labor so that the indigent would not become social drones.

In planning to undertake a major role in giving relief to the needy, the Bethel Relief Association began to systematize its own operation and even suggested the eventual consolidation of the cities' benevolent societies in a manner similar to the consolidation and systematizing of business enterprises. A general superintendent of relief was employed to examine each application and to keep careful records. All aid was channeled through his office after he had personally approved each request, as outlined by one of the Association's visitors. The distinction between worthy and unworthy poor remained an important criterion in determining eligibility for relief; and its concomitant, thorough investigation of the individual situation, was to become a keystone of the casework process.

During the late 1870's the Bethel Relief Association records contained frequent references to the London Charity Organization Society's attempts to centralize relief giving. In 1878 the annual report of the Association examined such developments in the London organization and suggested that Cleveland could attain comparable efficiency in the operation of charity work if there were a single organization in the city to investigate all requests for aid. As the idea began to take hold in Cleveland, a paper delivered to the National Conference of Charities and Corrections, which was held in the city in 1880, presented points relevant to establishing a central organization: pauperism was increasing and frauds were taking off with a large proportion of available assistance; indiscriminate charity was actually doing harm by encouraging idleness and improvidence; and little was being done to help the poor to help themselves.[4]

Trustees of the Bethel Union and the Bethel Relief Association were active in the move for a Charity Organization Society and anticipated that the Association might become the central organization. Already their registration process included the names of clients helped by the City Infirmary, so they had knowledge of most of the city's relief recipients. But there was opposition to such an arrangement because the "non-sectarian" Bethel agencies retained their Sunday School, a church in the Bethel building, and strong Protestant associations. Thus an independent Society for Organized Charity was formed in 1881, and it was not until 1884 that the Bethel Union relinquished the religious aspect of its work in preparation for a merger that created the Bethel Associated Charities.

The constitution of the Society for Organized Charity reflected past experiences and fresh plans for the future. The core of the new approach was to give relief to the deserving needy within an organizational framework that would protect the donors from deceit and duplication while at the same time reducing vagrancy and pauperism. The constitution specified the methods by which its aims were to be achieved:

1. By a system of registration to prevent imposture.
2. By securing cooperation among all charitable societies with this society and with each other.
3. By securing thorough investigation in every case.
4. By obtaining from existing agencies needed help.
5. By a system of personal visitation inducing self-respect, habits of thrift and better living.
6. By careful study of pauperism and the best means of preventing it.[5]

The new organization appointed as Superintendent, Henry N. Raymond, a businessman with a keen ear for publicity, who organized a city-wide drive to inform citizens of the new agency. City policemen were utilized to hand out 10,000 circulars urging householders not to give relief at the door but to send beggars to the Society's office for investigation and referral. Returns on questionnaires issued at the same time indicated that over 80 per cent of those responding had beggars calling at their doors. The Society and its successors waged a continuous campaign against street and house begging.

Superintendent Raymond, with paid employees of the Society, began to organize a registration system by recording in indexed books the names of all clients who received aid from the City Infirmary and the Bethel Relief Association, as well as names of charity patients in the city hospitals; but despite extensive publicity of the program most private agencies continued to give "indiscriminately" without referring to the central register. Furthermore, the Society found that many emergency cases came to its attention. Often clients with pressing needs could not wait for a careful investigation followed by further delay in referral to the appropriate agency. Within six months of its birth the Society was compelled to add the giving of direct relief to its functions.[6]

The merger of the Society with the Bethel agencies produced

new efforts to expand and systematize relief-giving. Board members of the new Bethel Associated Charities even tried, unsuccessfully, to persuade city officials to do away with tax-supported outdoor relief, which was considered the form of relief most damaging to the recipient's character. Renewed efforts were made to expand the central register of the enlarged agency, but the problem of securing interagency co-operation in this venture continued throughout the century.

The Depression of 1893 had a great influence on the development of private charity work in Cleveland. As the winter of that year approached, thousands of unemployed workers crowded the Bethel Associated Charities building seeking relief. It became clear that the existing organizational and financial arrangements were not adequate to meet the mounting problems. For some years past the district offices of the BAC had coincided with the political or the health divisions of the city. To meet growing relief problems with greater efficiency the number of offices was reduced to twelve. Physicians, who had formerly been committee chairmen supervising BAC operations from their offices in each district, were replaced by prominent businessmen who set up a separate office of the BAC in each of the twelve new divisions. Undoubtedly the new organization was based on the premise that businessmen would operate relief-giving with more efficiency and objectivity and less susceptibility to "improper influence." The BAC not only secured a paid investigator for each district but also enlisted the help of six hundred citizens experienced in charity work to serve on district committees. Each district operated with a considerable degree of independence—soliciting funds, buying and distributing supplies, and furnishing its own friendly visitors.[7]

The great need for relief funds produced a new city-wide fund-raising organization, the Citizens Relief Association, which, together with the district offices and their committees, raised $44,000. The local offices also secured great quantities of food, clothing, and fuel supplies for over 9,000 families who received help during the winter of 1893-94.

As a result of the success of the BAC in coping with the problems of the depression there were renewed efforts to strengthen the registration system and to abolish city-financed outdoor relief. The latter effort undoubtedly was based on concern that political considerations affected city relief. Pressure from the BAC did result in the establishment of a registration bureau in the city's Department of Charities and Corrections, but few of the other private charities in the city reported their relief expenditures to the new bureau.

Despite the fact that the BAC was able to meet extreme and pressing relief needs in 1893, the next ten years were difficult ones. Isolated members of the community began to suggest that concern for business-like efficiency and overemphasis on morality were preventing the needy from receiving help. Financial contributions lagged, demand for the agency's services grew with the increasing population of the city, and vigorous leadership was lacking. Superintendent Raymond resigned in 1898, noting that at times his work had been seriously handicapped by lack of funds. His successor, a kindly, elderly man who had been with the BAC for years, was in ill health for several years before his resignation in 1903. In 1900 the Bethel Associated Charities severed its last ties with the Bethel agencies and was reorganized to become the Associated Charities. Three years later, after a nationwide search for a man who could give leadership in the city, the board members of the Associated Charities found an experienced, energetic superintendent to give new direction to social work in Cleveland.[8]

James F. Jackson, who became the chief executive of the Associated Charities in 1904, was a former businessman who had been recruited into social work by Hastings H. Hart, the famous pioneer in social welfare. He was known for his organizational abilities and had held top executive posts in social work in Minnesota and New York. Although he recognized society's need to ameliorate destructive social conditions, he believed that the "chief concern of social work was to deal with individual disabilities."[9]

The community leaders who brought Jackson to the city anticipated that the Associated Charities would take a commanding role in the charitable movement in Cleveland. As the new superintendent moved to fulfill this aim, he ran into difficulty in finding trained and experienced social workers to expand his staff. From the beginning he carefully distinguished between trained workers and volunteers, and when he failed to secure trained staff members from eastern cities that already had educational programs for social work, he announced that he would open his own training program in the offices of the Associated Charities. With the support of influential members of the community he secured scholarships to a seven-month program for a small class of college graduates, who gained practical experience in the field at the same time that they were given lectures by Jackson and others experienced in social welfare. Recognizing that poverty had many causes, Jackson relied upon his paid trained workers to diagnose and deal constructively with individual problems of dependency and maladjustment. Volunteers, who were carefully chosen for the program of friendly visiting, worked under trained agency personnel. They did not give direct relief to families, although at times they offered valuable assistance in securing relief supplies for the agency. Rather, their role was to help improve the home situation of clients by showing steady friendly interest in the family and its problems. In the long run the most important aspect of the volunteer's work was the knowledge of broad social problems gained through firsthand experience. Equipped with such knowledge, volunteers played an important role in influencing powerful segments of the community to press for corrective social legislation and institutions. Under Jackson's leadership the function of casework gradually became the prime purpose of the trained workers, whereas securing community support became the most significant work of the volunteers.[10]

In endeavoring to build an organization of trained workers Jackson was aided by a progressive climate of opinion and a growing awareness that public and private social agencies were important tools for mastering the challenges of the modern urbanized society. During the first decade of the twentieth century Cleveland's population increased from 381,000 to 560,000, and in the public sector of the city men began to grapple with the problems produced by such urban expansion.

Tom L. Johnson, who was mayor of Cleveland from 1901 to 1909, gave the city dynamic political leadership during his tenure in office. This businessman-turned-politician was an intellectual captive of Henry George's belief that poverty, unemployment, slums, disease, and crime could be eliminated by destroying the privileged position of monopolists in land and business. In striving to make Cleveland a better place for the great mass of its citizens Johnson stimulated many local reformers and brought a number of them into leading positions in city government.

Johnson appointed Harris R. Cooley, a Presbyterian minister by profession and a sociologist by avocation, to head the Department of Charities and Corrections. Cooley believed that society was responsible for poverty, which was in turn the principal cause of crime. He agreed with Johnson that "the root of the evil must be destroyed, and that in the meantime delinquent men, women and children were to be cared for by the society that wronged them—not as objects of charity, but as fellow human beings who had been deprived of the opportunity to get on in the world." With this revolutionary view of public welfare, director Cooley made his department a model for the nation. For workhouse prisoners he instituted a more liberal parole system that provided for the release of hundreds of men. He secured authorization to purchase two thousand acres of land outside the city limits "where all the city's charges—the old, the sick, the young, and the delinquent—might be cared for" in pleasant surroundings that provided an opportunity for healthful work. On these lands the city built new institutions for the aged and infirm, for those suffering from tuberculosis, and for workhouse prisoners. Cooley also obtained a 285-acre farm in nearby Hudson, Ohio, on which he built eight cottages for the rehabilitation of delinquents sentenced by the Juvenile Court. The institution's school curriculum and supplementary classes in manual training and the care of livestock made the atmosphere more suggestive of a private school than of a reformatory.[11]

Cooley's approach toward the underprivileged was increasingly shared by many others in the community, especially those who supported and operated the settlement houses in the city. By 1909 there were nine settlement houses and neighborhood centers in Cleveland. Some of these, such as Hiram House and Goodrich

Settlement, were exceptionally influential, but all of them were actively engaged in providing neighborhood service in the fields of recreation, education, and character-building. Out of the settlement house movement grew new agencies. Baby clinics and milk stations were a natural outgrowth of the day nurseries which most of the settlements provided. For the crippled and the blind, agencies were developed to give those with physical defects educational training so that they might achieve some degree of independence and self-support. Educational classes for the foreign-born and their children led to the formation of discussion groups, and the Cleveland Public Library placed branches in most of the neighborhood centers. Although volunteer help was used extensively, all of the settlement houses had permanent, paid workers to supervise the volunteers. New interest in the constructive use of children's time led to an expansion of the city's public recreational facilities during Johnson's tenure in office. All public facilities had paid personnel in attendance.

With such rapid development of organizations and institutions it is not surprising that there was an increased demand for personnel equipped with the skills and knowledge necessary for successful operation of the new facilities. Many organizations followed the example of Associated Charities in providing training classes for those interested in such work. From the AC classes came social workers and administrators for the many new agencies and civic organizations that sprang up in the years before World War I. As the demand outstripped the supply, many educators and social workers began to explore the possibility of developing a school of social work.

Jackson had announced his interest in such an endeavor shortly after his arrival in Cleveland. He found a sympathetic listener in the person of Charles F. Thwing, president of Western Reserve University. In 1905 President Thwing held a meeting with Jackson and settlement house leaders "to consider the question of instruction in sociology in Cleveland." One result of the discussions which followed was the creation of the department of sociology at Western Reserve University in the fall of 1907. Although Jackson wanted a school of social work, at this time there was not sufficient support among university trustees for such an innovation. But Jackson secured a valuable ally for his quest when James E. Cutler came from the University of Michigan to fill the newly created Selah Chamberlain Chair of Sociology at Western Reserve. Cutler, who had studied under A. G. Keller at Yale and had been an assistant to William Graham Sumner, was to become one of the founders of the School of Applied Social Sciences and its dean for twenty-five years—a strange career for one whose mentor wrote that trenchant antireform essay, "The Absurd Effort to Make the World Over." Despite his educational background Cutler gradually rejected the strict social-Darwinist view of society in favor of the position of Peter Kropotkin, who stressed that man's capacity for co-operation was crucial to his survival.

Upon his arrival in Cleveland Cutler became active in many phases of social work outside of his university teaching. His increased contact with the social and civic problems of the city convinced him that there was an excellent opportunity for Western Reserve University to build a school of social service. He envisioned a school that would train students for careers in many areas of public administration as well as for the field of social work. He even cited the country's recent acquisition of colonies to point up the need for trained colonial administrators.

As early as 1908 committees of university and social agency executives were appointed to explore the possibility of establishing a school, but the first outcome of these discussions was limited to evening extension courses in practical sociology for those interested in social work and for members of the Visiting Nurse Association. Public interest in these courses demonstrated the educational needs of many engaged in social work and related fields. One hundred people attended the first class, and over sixty students enrolled for the full course, to which Cutler invited prominent local and national social workers and reformers to discuss their work as well as the social and civic problems that faced the community and the nation. Within the formal structure of the university Cutler selected four seniors from the College of Women to become students in a laboratory course which provided at least six hours per week of work in social work agencies. William J. Norton, a social worker at Goodrich House, was enlisted to serve as field supervisor for the course.

In a letter to President Thwing in May, 1909, Cutler again pressed Western Reserve to establish a school of social science. He argued that "the removal of the University from Hudson to Cleveland had determined the fact that its work must be governed by other considerations than those which apply to educational institutions in rural districts. Clearly Western Reserve is now a city university and must accept the responsibilities of such an institution. The policy of the broadest possible direct service to the community should be the settled policy of the University and it should be followed to its logical consequences; it should under no circumstances be abandoned."[12]

From 1905 until 1913 most members of the university community took a cautious and conservative view of the idea of establishing a professional school for social work within the confines of their educational institution. The president and a few of the trustees were sympathetic, but most members of the faculty were far more anxious to secure the establishment of a separate graduate school than a school for a new profession.

There were, however, other forces operating within the city to lend support to a school of social work. The business community, operating through the Chamber of Commerce, shared some of the prevailing interest in local reforms. Various committees of the Chamber investigated and secured legislation to improve public health and housing conditions in Cleveland. In the area of social work Chamber members who were leaders in various charity organizations succeeded in establishing a Chamber Committee on Benevolent Associations "to foster and support the useful charities and to discourage . . . and eliminate those which were found to be unworthy of confidence." This committee was one response to the proliferation of charities that had accompanied the rapid growth of the city. Many of the newer ones, lacking the support of the established community, engaged in aggressive and sometimes wasteful fund-raising drives that often cost more than the net charitable gain. The community that had tried unsuccessfully to secure a system of registration for relief clients now embarked upon a system of registration for charitable societies with the avowed purpose of distinguishing between worthy and unworthy institutions.

When the Committee on Benevolent Associations was established in 1900, its members considered two possible courses of action: (1) "The careful investigation of Cleveland's benevolent institutions by the committee and the endorsement of those whose work and financial methods merit approval and support." (2) "The collection and the distribution by the committee of all money contributed for the benevolent institutions of the city." The second course of action was discarded as unfeasible, but after a few short years the Committee was able to report to the Chamber of Commerce that "most associations found it necessary to secure the endorsement card of the Committee in order to get funds."[13]

The second proposal was a logical sequence to the first, but it was a number of years before Cleveland achieved an integrated agency for collection and distribution of charitable funds. The pioneering step in the federating of social agencies was taken by Cleveland's Jewish community in 1903. Jewish charities had also proliferated as thousands of Jews from Eastern Europe flooded into Cleveland in the latter part of the nineteenth century. To avoid unnecessary duplication the Jewish community pressed successfully for a federated agency similar to the program that had been considered by the Committee on Benevolent Associations. Ten years later in 1913 the Cleveland Federation for Charity and Philanthropy was organized to co-ordinate the fund raising of the various participating agencies.

One of the most important results of community organizations which scrutinized agencies' budgets and activities was the establishment of certain standards of operation. Many agencies that were put on probation for failing to meet standards of administration or performance turned to Jackson of Associated Charities for advice and assistance. This development further increased the demand for trained personnel and intensified the pressure for a school to train social workers.

In May of 1911 A. B. Williams, an executive of the Humane Society, prepared a memo for President Thwing in which he called upon the university to establish courses of training in social work, municipal administration, and public health work. He asserted "that there is a great opportunity . . . for the University to identify itself with the life of the community and to occupy a place of leadership in matters affecting the common welfare. It can give direction and definiteness to the entire social program here, if it is able to enthuse and inspire those who are doing the work, and why shouldn't it?"[14]

But it was another two years before those interested in establishing a school began to make headway. In February of 1913 President Thwing called a meeting of representatives of various agencies to discuss the question. A subcommittee which was appointed at this meeting reported back to the General Committee on a School for Social Service with the recommendation that such a school be established under the auspices of Western Reserve University. Under the subcommittee proposal students would undertake a two-year course requiring a college degree for admittance. University instructors would give course work in conjunction with a heavy schedule of practical work to be conducted under the supervision of the staff of various local social agencies. The subcommittee noted that there was an obvious need for such a school since at that time nine organizations were providing special training courses for their workers.

President Thwing presided at a second meeting on the subject in October of 1913. After the need for a school of social work had been reiterated Thwing suggested that the group present be organized "to aid and promote a program of sociological instruction by articulating, consolidating and unifying" the existing programs of instruction. At a subsequent meeting a subcommittee reported a recommendation to incorporate "The School for Public Service and Research." The proposed purposes of the school were (1) to promote, establish, and maintain research studies for the discovery and proper understanding of the various factors in the problem of human welfare and public betterment; and (2) to promote and provide such instruction as might be deemed helpful to the most effective treatment of that problem.[15]

President Thwing presided at a public meeting called to discuss the proposed school. Among those who participated in the discussion were the Rev. Harris R. Cooley, President Charles S. Howe of Case School of Applied Sciences, Professor Walter T. Dunmore of Western Reserve's law school, Dr. A. R. Warner of Lakeside Hospital and Western Reserve's medical school, and Martin A. Marks, a prominent businessman and president of the newly organized Cleveland Federation for Charity and Philanthropy. The consensus of the meeting was that such a school should be established under the auspices of Western Reserve University.

Dr. Warner, James F. Jackson, and Martin A. Marks were appointed to draw up a petition to be presented to the trustees of WRU. The petition was a flattering document designed to appeal to the pride and local patriotism of the men who governed the largest university between Chicago and New York:

> Representing the will and wishes of eighteen philanthropic organizations of Cleveland, we respectfully present the following for your consideration.
>
> For at least ten years there has been a growing conviction among the various public welfare workers that there was in Cleveland a need and an opportunity for a school to teach sociologic sciences . . . . The recent increased demand for public and social service workers and the scarcity of tutored or practically trained candidates for these positions has compelled philanthropic organizations to give temporary courses of instruction that their workers might at least be partially trained; however, such courses have uniformly proven entirely inadequate and no other result was ever expected. This condition and the constant stream of applications from high grade, educated and suitable but entirely untrained persons for positions to do any and all kinds of social work has made these pleas for such a school more numerous and more emphatic.
>
> . . . .
>
> Cleveland with its great and varied business activities, its cosmopolitan population and its rapid growth is a fitting place to teach the sociologic sciences and to train in social work. . . . [No] city has on the whole more advanced, varied or active philanthropic institutions, municipal or private, or more efficient fabric of social organizations working for the common welfare. . . . Therefore, no city offers greater opportunity for desirable practical experience, for popular extension courses, for properly supervised survey or original research work. . . . Between New York and Chicago there is no university which now has the talent in the various medical, legal,

philosophical, sociologic and economic branches already in its organization to combine and assemble for such a school in any way
equal to that at Reserve. Reserve has the necessary standing and
prestige to attract properly prepared students to sociologic courses
carrying university credits and leading to degrees. Reserve also has
the confidence and the friendship of every social institution of
Cleveland, so that practical extension courses could be given in co-
operation with each and all of such institutions, and opportunity
given to prepare for any special field of work. Such a combination
of courses, academic, practical, liberal, would we believe, constitute
a school in harmony with, but in advance of, the recent trend of
sociologic teaching and one more popular, because more practical
and of more value to promote public welfare, than the older established conventional schools of philanthropy.[16]

But the trustees of Western Reserve University were still hesi-
tant, still concerned that training for "a few" was "not in accord
with the function of a University." Furthermore, there was the
difficult question of financing the school. In outlining the needs
of a school of social service Cutler estimated that it would require
a minimum endowment of at least $500,000, and if it were to
achieve its greatest efficiency, at least $1,000,000. The trustees ap-
pointed a committee composed of Frederick H. Goff, Malcolm L.
McBride, and William H. Baldwin to investigate the proposal and
report their findings.

During 1914, while the trustees were studying the proposal, a
depression struck Cleveland that left thousands of citizens unemployed. The demand for assistance was so great that the Associated Charities and the Outdoor Relief Department of the city ran
out of funds. Soup kitchens made their appearance on the downtown streets for the first time since the depression of 1893. The city
council called upon the newly organized Cleveland Foundation,
which had been founded by Frederick H. Goff, to "investigate public and private relief agencies looking to any possible increase in
efficiency, means of economy, methods of greater service and
plans for correlating the various resources and agencies." One of
the findings of this investigation was that there was a great need
for more and better-trained social workers to staff the agencies
under study.[17]

Meanwhile resistance to the school within the university was
weakening. Professor Cutler broadened his concept of a profes-

sional school to include "a graduate school that shall undertake to give preparatory training not only for teaching but for other forms of public service as well." He asserted that "practically all of the graduate work which might be given by the departments of economics, political science and sociology would become a part of the curriculum of a school of public service and in addition the curricula of the schools of medicine and of law would be drawn upon, particularly the newer extensions of their curricula."[18] For the Visiting Nurse Association Cutler had already organized University extension courses, for which members of the sociology and history departments and the school of medicine were giving lectures. Cutler's interest in other forms of public service training was also very attractive to Professor A. H. Hatton of the political science department. Hatton was a leading municipal reformer in the city and was an ardent advocate of improving the qualiy of municipal government by introducing modern methods of administration.

Undoubtedly the improved climate of opinion regarding the proposed school contributed to the subcommittee's decision to return a favorable report to the Board of Trustees. On October 24, 1914, the governing body of Western Reserve University authorized the establishment of the School of Social Science and Research.

NOTES

[1] Florence T. Waite, *A Warm Friend for the Spirit: A History of the Family Service Association of Cleveland and Its Forebears, 1830-1952* (Cleveland: Family Service Association, 1960), 1. Because the history of SASS and that of Associated Charities were so closely interwoven for many years, Miss Waite's book is a valuable guide, and I am deeply in her debt.

[2] Philip Klein, "Social Work," *Encyclopedia of Social Science*, ed. E. R. A. Seligman (New York: Macmillan Co., 1934), XIV, 165.

[3] Waite, 11.

[4] *Ibid.*, 19-23.

[5] *Ibid.*, 28-29.

[6] *Ibid.*, 36-37.

[7] *Ibid.*, 61-63.

8 See Frederick C. Howe, *Confessions of a Reformer* (New York: Charles Scribner & Sons, 1925), 78-79, for a forthright criticism of the business-like approach of the AC.

9 Clara A. Kaiser, "Organized Social Work in Cleveland, Its History and Setting" (Unpublished Ph.D. dissertation, The Ohio State University, 1936), 138. Miss Kaiser, who taught at SASS from 1927 to 1934, has made many perceptive comments in this dissertation. Her analysis of organizational developments in social work during the 1920's and early 1930's is a solid contribution to social work history.

10 Waite, 83-88.

11 Tom L. Johnson, *My Story*, ed. Elizabeth J. Hauser (New York: B. W. Huebsch, 1915), 173-79.

12 James E. Cutler to Charles F. Thwing, May 14, 1909.

13 Kaiser, 160-63.

14 A. B. Williams, "Memorandum for President Thwing," May, 1911.

15 "Statement of History of Movement for School," James E. Cutler Papers.

16 "Petition Addressed to Board of Trustees, Western Reserve University," December 18, 1913.

17 Nathaniel R. Howard, *Trust For All Time* (Cleveland: The Cleveland Foundation, 1963), 17-18.

18 James E. Cutler to Charles F. Thwing, March 15, 1913.

The Making of a School

The three trustees who had reported favorably on the proposal for a new school of social work were again enlisted by the Board of Trustees to begin laying plans for the school. One of them, William H. Baldwin, was especially interested in the project. He began his investigation by consulting with Allen T. Burns, who had directed the recently completed Cleveland Foundation survey of social and public agencies. Burns believed that the new school should be headed by a person who was a "master of apprentices," capable of doing the same work the students would be studying in field placement. Although he thought that it would be helpful if such a man were also capable of lecturing on academic subjects, he asserted that the previously established schools in New York and Chicago were not giving their students sufficient practical training.[1]

Baldwin, who was not convinced by Burns's argument, traveled to New York to consult with such leaders in social service as John M. Glenn, member of the board of trustees of the New York School of Philanthropy and general director of the Russell Sage Foundation, and Miss Mary E. Richmond, noted social worker and director of the Charity Organization Department of the Russell Sage Foundation. Both Glenn and Miss Richmond stressed the need for the new school to obtain a good administrator, rather than a master of apprentices, to lead its program. In a long conference with Baldwin Miss Richmond urged that the school concentrate on "fundamental instructions in the general principles which underlie social work, rather than training in the various specialties which grow out of it, like charity organization work, and playground work and institutional work." Neither Miss Richmond nor Glenn was able to recommend anyone for the chairmanship of Cleveland's new school, and Baldwin came to the conclusion that it would be best to find a local man for the position. (Miss Richmond was considered by the committee, but they came to the conclusion that the chairmanship needed the stronger personality of a man—they didn't know Mary E. Richmond very well.)

While he was in New York Baldwin arranged a meeting with Cutler and J. B. Chamberlain, a trustee of WRU who had given substantial financial support to the sociology department. Cutler, who was on a leave of absence, was doing research in the East because the outbreak of World War I had forced him to cancel a trip to Germany. During the consultation with Cutler the two trustees were impressed with the young sociology professor, who suggested that the department of sociology might undertake the organization and conduct of the new school if the trustees were not able to find a man to head it. Baldwin wrote to Thwing that Cutler was "quiet, thoughtful and clear-headed." Recognizing the difficulty in finding someone to take charge of the school because the field was new and had not yet produced a trained body of teachers, the subcommittee recommended Cutler's appointment to the Board of Trustees.[2]

As soon as Cutler was authorized to organize the new school, he proceeded to get advice from his colleagues at Reserve, his associates in various civic and public organizations, and leaders in the social work field from Cleveland and the East. He presented his first report to President Thwing in January of 1915. The name that Cutler advocated for the new institution, The School of Applied Social Sciences, reflected his own conviction that the school should be oriented toward the scientific application of the principles discovered in the sociologic sciences. Some community leaders considered this name pretentious. Frederick A. Blossom declared that such a name would leave the impression that "we who are trying to give philanthropy a substantial basis are reducing it to the ashes of dead, cold 'science.'" The president of Case School of Applied Science feared that the new school would be confused with his next-door institution. But there were objections to nearly all of the suggested names. In the end Cutler prevailed, and the new school was officially christened the School of Applied Social Sciences.

Cutler's report to the president went on to outline a two-year graduate program consisting of a general lecture curriculum along with carefully supervised field work. Cutler anticipated that in the second year of study seminars would largely replace lecture courses. The faculty was to be drawn from the Reserve staff, supplemented by special lecturers and instructors who were active in various fields of social and public service. Student supervisors for the field work program would be carefully chosen from the staffs of social agencies.

Cutler planned four general divisions within the school: (1) Family Welfare and Social Service, (2) Civics and Public Service, (3) Public Health Nursing, and (4) Play and Recreation. He recognized that there were other important areas, such as child welfare, penal and correctional agencies, and church social work; but he felt that neither the university faculty nor the agencies in these fields were yet equipped to provide proper instruction and training for students.

In his report Cutler submitted a list of courses to be offered to students in each division of the school along with a list of instructors available for the program. He gave special attention to the fact that every social worker with whom he had conferred had stressed the importance of courses in psychology. Already Western Reserve was offering a course in the general principles of psychology and in the College for Women had a specialist in educational psychology. Cutler pointed out the special need in the School of Applied Social Sciences to have a specialist in the areas of clinical and experimental psychology. He quoted Dr. Richard C. Cabot, a pioneer in the field of medical social work, who urged that social workers learn to apply psychological principles "to the treatment of character under adversity," and he pointed out that social workers, unlike lawyers and doctors, could not refuse to take a case but must learn to deal with "all sorts and conditions of men." He concluded that it would be a real contribution to Cleveland if the School of Applied Social Sciences could bring to its faculty a specialist in experimental and clinical psychology.

In discussing the program of practical training Cutler urged that experienced persons well acquainted with the work of their agencies be placed on the school staff to supervise students. He insisted that practical training does not consist in sending students to organizations to observe and pick up what they can, nor does it consist in sending students on their own responsibility and with general instructions to make investigations of one sort or another. Students ought to observe under the eye of a competent director who has had executive and administrative experience and to practice under the direction of one whose principal object is that of teaching and instructing rather than getting a certain amount of work done.

Cutler proposed admission requirements and degrees for several classes of students. Students in the division of Public Health Nursing were to be graduates of nurses' training schools of good standing. Preferably they would have some experience in nursing before coming to the school, and they would receive a certificate after completing a one-year course of training. In the other three divisions of the School of Applied Social Sciences there were to be two general categories for admission and degrees. Students with an A.B. degree would be admitted to the school and would receive an A.M. degree upon successful completion of the two-year program. Within this category Cutler also provided for the possibility of admitting well-qualified undergraduates in their senior year so that they could complete their masters' degrees just one year after receiving the A.B. degree. Programs similar to this were available within Western Reserve's medical school and law school. Cutler also provided a special category of admission for mature and experienced students, who could take single courses for fees charged on a pro rata basis. Such students would be entitled to receive certificates after completing one or two years of work.

The School was to be open to both men and women for a tuition fee of $125 a year. Cutler noted that this amount might prove a hardship to some students but suggested that agencies in need of trained workers might choose students to receive scholarships in return for commitments by the students to work in those agencies after graduation.

Before concluding this lengthy report, Cutler suggested that the School make provision in its budget for lectures and extension courses that would be open to members of the Cleveland community to "promote thought and discussion upon questions of social and public interest."

Although Cutler's report was well received by the trustees, they decided that in light of the problem of financing the School "it was unwise to start . . . until an adequate income was provided." Earlier a subcommittee on the School had estimated that a minimum of $4,400 a year would be needed to operate the new institution. With the able support of President Thwing, Cutler turned his attention to securing funds from patrons in the community. By November they had secured nearly one thousand dollars, along with additional pledges of ten thousand dollars for each of the following five years. These funds were in addition to the anticipated tuition-fee income. Such a financial base was a far cry from the minimum endowment of one-half million dollars recommended by Cutler two years earlier, but nevertheless the trustees authorized Western Reserve University to open the School of Applied Social Sciences in the fall of 1916. In December of 1915 James E. Cutler was appointed the School's first dean.

The founding of the School of Applied Social Sciences at this time was an act of faith and an expression of hope for both trustees and faculty. The whole concept of social work as a profession had come under heavy attack in 1915 when Abraham Flexner, an expert on education, told the National Conference of Charities and Corrections that social work did not meet the qualifications for a profession that he had used for his 1910 study of the field of medicine.

Cutler, who was convinced that the School must play an important role in social welfare in the city, spent a great deal of time conferring and corresponding with community leaders in the areas for which the School would accept students. The response was enthusiastic, but most of his community contacts took a narrow view of the educational aspects of the new School.

James F. Jackson, the most important social worker in Cleveland, stressed the need for every student to take a Charity Organization Society course during his first year at the School. Such a course was to be supplemented by regular work in one of the district offices of Associated Charities. In the beginning such a student would be assigned tasks such as those performed by a "thoroughly dependable volunteer," and gradually the student's

responsibility would be increased according to the ability which
he demonstrated. Jackson, however, anticipated that applicants
for social work positions at Associated Charities would continue
with their studies at the agency after they finished at SASS. He
thought that Associated Charities would benefit by being able to
"select the more promising students for admission to [their] training classes." He conceded that students who had graduated from
the School would be able to omit some parts of AC's training program because they would already be acquainted with the elements
of Associated Charities work and be familiar with the city. Graduates of SASS who were accepted for employment by AC "would
begin on [the] payroll where other people would be at the end
of seven months."[3]

Such emphasis upon practical work was echoed by Howell
Wright, superintendent of City Hospital, when he criticized an
outline of proposed courses sent to him by Cutler. He protested
that there were "too many lectures in theory and textbook stuff,"
and he called for the inclusion of more field work. He also hoped
that students would become more acquainted with public welfare
because "so many institutions are turning out people whose minds
are poisoned with the idea that all social work is done by private
institutions, with the result that they are not interested in public
administration except to criticize it and its most conspicuous fail-
ures."

On the other hand, Dr. A. R. Warner, who had been very active
in the move to establish a school, warned that Cutler must be
careful that field practice did not become the simple routine work
of the agency to which the student had been assigned. While he
recognized that in the first year the School's program "must be
largely determined by the material and machinery taken over," he
urged that Cutler "make social work a profession to be learned by
thought and study, instead of a trade to be learned by purely practical experience."

Although the settlement-house workers did not participate ac-
tively in these discussions about the shape and form of the School,
Cutler did consult with Starr Cadwallader, former director of
Goodrich House, and with members of the public recreation agen-

cies. Cadwallader stressed the importance of courses in public administration and the need for better understanding of the feebleminded. He asserted that "the case method of teaching is too narrow in scope and application to serve as a basis for establishing a profession—the rehabilitation of a family and of individual members of the family is not the only kind of case to be studied." Cadwallader called for the development of community case work and neighborhood case work, but unfortunately he did not detail his thinking about these fields. T. M. Black, Commissioner of Recreation for the city, did present a rough outline of the courses which might be included in plans for the School's Division of Play and Recreation.

In planning for the Division of Public Administration, Cutler received detailed suggestions from the chairmen of Western Reserve's departments of political science and economics. Professor C. C. Arbuthnot of the economics department advised courses in money, banking, public finances, trusts, railways, and foreign trade for the field of public administration; and he also suggested that social work students be given courses in socialism and labor problems. Professor Arbuthnot also considered the financing of such education. He estimated a total cost of $2,500 a year—$1,500 to $1,800 for the economics department and the remainder for courses to be developed by the departments of political science and history.

Professor A. R. Hatton of the political science department prepared an outline of courses which he believed were important if the Division of Public Administration were to train students for positions in the broad field of public service: secretaries of civic organizations; municipal and state commissioners; legislative experts; and civil servants in local, state, and national government posts. He stressed the need for students to receive practical work and research in addition to theoretical courses. He believed that credit should be given for properly supervised field experience in civic organizations, bureaus of research, and governmental departments. Hatton also pointed out the importance of a good research library. While he believed that the existing political science library was adequate for present use, he estimated that the new

School would need additional books costing at least two thousand dollars per year.

The proposed Division of Public Health Nursing presented few problems for Cutler. The sociology department had been responsible for special courses for public health nurses since 1911. The existing program was to be incorporated into the new School under the supervision of Cecilia A. Evans, the nursing director, who was to become a full-time member of the university faculty. Graduates of the one-year course who were also college graduates were to be eligible to continue for masters' degrees in public health administration.

Although community leaders gave freely of their time and advice in making suggestions about the content of courses in the new School, they left the university with the burden of financing the endeavor. Operating funds for the first year of the School were secured from a number of prominent Clevelanders, who contributed between $100 and $2,500, and from private and public health agencies in the city, which supported the Division of Public Health Nursing. The total budget for the academic year 1916-17 was estimated at $9,280. Not one of the social agencies or the welfare federations in the city contributed to the support of the School. Instead, the university found itself contributing to the Associated Charities by taking over the cost of AC's training class. Had the faculty members of the sociology, political science, and economics departments not contributed their services to SASS without compensation, it is doubtful that the School would have opened in the fall of 1916.

The School started with a general faculty of twenty-one: seven were appointed by the university to SASS, nine were members of established departments of the university, and five were instructors in the University Public Health Nursing District. The student body consisted of thirty-five: fifteen were designated as regular students, and the remainder were designated as special students ("persons of liberal education and practical experience . . . [taking] . . . particular courses in which they have special interest, without reference to the attainment of a degree").

Of the three divisions* of the School of Applied Social Sciences it was the Division of Health Administration that made the most progress for the first few years, and, indeed, pioneered in the education of public health nurses. The Visiting Nurse Association had been experimenting with training methods for a number of years before the program became a part of the new School. Belle Sherwin, who was one of the founders of the association, believed that the hospital-trained nurse needed additional courses in social work before she was qualified to do public health nursing:

> The visiting nurse has been transported at least half a hemisphere from her hospital when she enters the home of her typical patient, though he may live only a few blocks from the hospital door. To disorder, darkness, bad air and overcrowded space are added the customs and standards of a foreign peasant. The situation requires immediately a whole new world of reading, thinking and understanding, in addition to a new method of treatment which shall embrace the family and its surroundings, and it calls for an initiative which has been trained out of the hospital nurse. The physical care of the patient of the visiting nurse cannot be divorced from the consideration of his social and economic condition.[4]

In the fall of 1917 the School of Applied Social Sciences, working in close co-operation with the city Division of Health and several private health agencies, took charge of a section of one of the city's health districts. The School's Division of Public Health Nursing placed members of its teaching staff in a central office which housed the various health clinics. The teaching district, an area in which 60,000 people of sixteen different nationalities lived in poor housing, became a laboratory for the student, who was under careful supervision. This laboratory experience took place only after the student nurse had spent one semester taking courses in social work and field work at Associated Charities.

The success of this program was highlighted by the 1920 Cleveland Foundation Hospital and Health Survey, a study which was extremely critical of the inadequate health services in the city. The foundation report noted: "The students are, in fact, receiving thorough practice in public health nursing; the patients are receiv-

---

* The Division of Play and Recreation never materialized, although students in SASS could and did take such courses in other schools of the university.

ing a very excellent quality of nursing service." Until the middle
of the 1920's the Division of Public Health Nursing dominated the
School in terms of the number of students and the size of the budget, but after that time the education of social workers became the
major role of the School. The Public Health Nursing Division remained part of SASS until 1939, when it was transferred to the
Frances Payne Bolton School of Nursing of Western Reserve University.

The Division of Public Administration, for which there were
high hopes in the early years of the School, never developed into
a significant part of the new institution. When SASS opened in
1916, Professor Hatton, Professor Arbuthnot, and Professor Raymond Moley offered courses in municipal government and administration, labor problems, socialism, and American government;
and Hatton and a new instructor in political science, H. C.
Hodges, gave an evening extension course on city and county government for public employees. But the Division had only two full-
time students; and despite the fact that the extension courses were
well-attended, Cutler reported to President Thwing that they
were "not notably successful." The plan of securing field-work
placement for students in various civic and public organizations
was never developed.

Hatton, who had been a leading advocate of the Division, suffered a prolonged illness during the first year of the School, and
in the following year the National Short Ballot Organization obtained his services for a half-time position which severely cut into
his time at SASS. Furthermore the entry of the United States into
World War I diverted attention from domestic problems, and the
draft cut off the supply of potential candidates for the Division of
Public Administration. The teaching staff, which had been working without compensation, was called upon by local authorities to
assist in numerous wartime activities and could not devote the
time necessary to develop programs for SASS.

In 1919 one student was awarded a master's degree in public
administration, but various efforts to reactivate the Division during the 1920's never succeeded. The last major attempt was made
in 1927 during the period when Cleveland was operating under

the city-manager plan of government. The fact that Cleveland, the largest city in the nation to adopt this form of government, had done so stimulated civic reformers, especially A. R. Hatton, to try to revive the moribund Division of Public Administration. Hatton was assured of City Manager William R. Hopkins' co-operation in establishing training programs for students, and he even secured a commitment that the International City Managers Association would locate in Cleveland if the university would house the organization and develop a school of public administration. George A. Eastman of Rochester, New York, offered to contribute $25,000 a year for five years, a sum which the City Managers Association promised to match. Eastman, however, wanted to establish the school under an independent board of trustees—a condition that the university was not willing to accept. Hatton left Cleveland to go to Northwestern University shortly thereafter, and the idea of training personnel for public administration was not developed until the 1960's when a revitalized political science department instituted an advanced program in that field.

Despite the exciting talk about establishing a graduate program in social work education which would provide, in conjunction with the university's social science departments, an integrated body of knowledge to serve as the basis for the professional practice of social work, the development of such an approach was very slow. When the School opened, the Division of Family Welfare and Social Service was the "Associated Charities training course dressed up in academic garb."[5] James F. Jackson, who remained the superintendent of Associated Charities, was appointed director of the Division. Two other staff members, who had been conducting the AC training class, were appointed faculty members of SASS, with the responsibility of teaching the only course offered to students in the Division. These two faculty members were paid by Associated Charities, which was in turn reimbursed by the School. Those interested in the program applied to and were accepted by the agency, which provided a classroom and office in the AC building and paid students a stipend to cover their living expenses. In the early years part or all of the student's tuition was frequently paid by the agency. As the demand for trained workers increased, it was the Associated Charities which engaged in successive programs of recruitment for the School.

During the first year of the School's operation students in the Division of Family Welfare and Social Service took a course in Casework with Families which met for one hour every day during the first six weeks and for one hour three times a week for the rest of the semester. The course "covered the essential points in Charity Organization Society history, investigation, cooperation and treatment. To enlarge the students' appreciation of practical cooperation there were seventeen talks given by representatives from other organizations in which emphasis was put on the functions of these organizations and their relationship to Associated Charities." These talks covered such topics as housing conditions, prison reform, vocational guidance, and industrial problems. During the second year of the School this course was expanded to include two semesters of classroom work with more "intensive study of social diagnosis and case treatment" and more emphasis on the role of the social worker in relation to social reforms. It was not until 1920 that a second-year course was added to the program, and not until 1924 that Western Reserve University awarded social workers the first degrees of Master in Social Administration.

The remainder of the social worker's education was in field work in the agency, a program which Dean Cutler considered analogous to laboratory courses given in the physical sciences. Students were regarded as junior staff members and worked the same hours as other members of the staff except for the three to five hours per week spent in the Casework with Families course. Early field work consisted of visiting clients with senior staff members. After reading and summarizing the records of some of the families, the students began to assume direct responsibility for them. The students' handling of their cases was often examined and discussed in the Casework class.

The School of Applied Social Sciences had been in operation for less than one year when the United States entered World War I on April 7, 1917. The national emergency that followed interrupted the nascent plans for the new graduate school at a crucial

period in its development. The faculty of the university responded
to the crisis by declaring that they were willing to make any contribution to aid the cause of democracy—even suspension of the
university's entire educational program. Although such a drastic
move was not deemed necessary by the federal government, many
faculty members, including a large number of those who had been
involved in planning curriculum for SASS, devoted large amounts
of their time to aiding the war effort on the local and national
scenes. For example, Raymond Moley of the political science department became director of the city's Americanization Board,
which directed a program designed to hasten the national identification of thousands of Cleveland's foreign-born residents. After
pondering the question of how to serve his country and consulting
with a number of people, Dean Cutler decided to enlist. He served
in the Military Intelligence Division and the Morale Branch of
the Chief of Staff Office in Washington, D.C.

There was rapid recognition of the need for an expanded wartime program at Associated Charities, which had had a foretaste
of the domestic consequences of war in 1916 during the trouble
on the Mexican border. When the local chapter of the Red Cross
had been unable to meet the needs of families of the Ohio National Guard troops, who were called up for the emergency, the
AC had stepped in to provide relief and casework service for
these families. In his first annual report as director of the Division
of Family Welfare and Social Science, Jackson focused on the fact
that "because of the present national crisis and the universal need
for people skilled in giving case treatment, there is a great demand
for trained workers who are farseeing and equipped to contend
with the steadily falling standards of living incident to the war
conditions." As a result, the School, in conjunction with Associated
Charities, turned its attention to organizing training classes for
Red Cross volunteers. This six-week course, which was based on
a similar program developed by the New York School of Philanthropy, consisted of two class hours each week and field work assignments in the district offices of Associated Charities. Those who
completed the work satisfactorily and passed an examination were
awarded a certificate by the School. At the request of the Civilian

Relief Department of the American Red Cross, the School also established a Red Cross Home Institute to train those who were to become executive secretaries of the Red Cross in small communities in the Great Lakes area. The institute curriculum was derived from the School's casework class. Another program to train volunteers in emergency service was developed at the request of local defense committees.

This increase in training programs for Red Cross workers during the war resulted in several temporary postwar courses. In 1919 the demand for training for workers in other agencies encouraged the School to open a class on the theory and technique of casework for those doing social work throughout the city. This was a noncredit course which was held at the Associated Charities building in the late afternoon so that those employed in agencies would not lose time from their work. In 1921 the School and the Lake Division of the Red Cross co-operated in offering an institute for advanced training in the peacetime work of the Red Cross. Thirty Red Cross secretaries enrolled in a six-week course which included content in family casework, community organization, public health, and social administration.

The first major program developed by the School of Applied Social Sciences after the war was "a child welfare training course such as existed in the family field." For some years, particularly since the Western Reserve Conference on the Care of Neglected and Dependent Children held in 1910, there had been growing concern in Cleveland about child welfare. Following the conference a Council on Child Welfare was organized to achieve better co-ordination among the various agencies active in the field. When the Federation for Charities and Philanthropy was organized in 1914, the council became a constituent part of the new organization under the name of the Cleveland Child Welfare Council.

In 1917 this council undertook a study of the problem of dependent and delinquent children in the city. The findings of the study clearly indicated the inadequacies of existing institutions, and the report recommended the establishment of a central clearing house for all institutions and placement organizations serving children. At this time one of the benefactors of SASS considered founding

a chair in child welfare, but the difficulty of finding a person qualified for the position and diversion of community attention to the
war effort foreclosed this move.

The war and the influenza epidemics of 1918 and 1919 so over-
crowded the institutions for dependent children that in 1920 the
Cleveland Welfare Federation decided to conduct a thorough survey of the child welfare field under the direction of Dr. Henry W.
Thurston of the New York School of Social Work. The results
pointed up serious defects in many of the child-care institutions—
unsanitary equipment, poor physical arrangements, and inadequate medical care for the children. Furthermore, Dr. Thurston
discovered that many of the children had at least one parent or
other adult members of their families still living. Such placements
were in direct violation of the principles established by the 1910
conference, which had stressed the importance of rearing children
in their own homes, if possible, or in foster homes when removal
was necessary. Another section of the survey emphasized the need
for training for the personnel of child-care agencies.

As a result of this survey a new organization, the Children's Bureau, was established in 1921 to act as a central bureau of investigation for all child-care agencies in the county. The demand for
trained personnel stimulated the new Children's Bureau and the
Humane Society, a large child-care agency, to petition the School
of Applied Social Sciences to establish a program in child welfare.
In the fall of 1921 the School introduced a one-year course in response to this request. Miss Maud Morlock, who had attended
Chicago's School of Civics and Philanthropy, was appointed to
the faculty of SASS to direct the course in child welfare, and the
two petitioning agencies furnished field placements for students.
Although there were more agencies which requested students,
only two others were granted permission to participate in the
training program—on condition that for six months, students attached to the two other agencies would be placed at the Humane
Society and the Children's Bureau, where the School felt there
were better arrangements for supervised training.

The purpose of the child welfare course taught by Miss Morlock
was "to give a solid foundation in the theory and the principles of

casework and of child welfare with discussion of such problems as the students were meeting in their field work." The course included lectures by outside specialists in child welfare and allied fields. Three years after the program was initiated, Miss Morlock reported the need for more than four hours a week in the classroom and pointed out that "in order to appreciate the problems pertaining to children a solid foundation of the underlying principles must be laid and considerably more instruction should be given in child psychology and psychiatry." This was the first time that a member of the social work faculty at SASS stressed the importance of strengthening the academic program.

In 1923 the child welfare course was extended to two years, and a year later a master's degree was awarded to the first student of child welfare. Under Miss Morlock's direction there were a number of extension courses developed in child welfare to meet pressing needs in community agencies. A course in child training and parental education was offered to practicing caseworkers. Later the School co-operated with an educational psychologist from the Cleveland School of Education to open a course in child training for parents. In 1923 Miss Morlock initiated a course in Community Resources for a group of staff workers from children's institutions in the community. The acute problems of these institutions later led to an attempt to provide a two-year training course in the administration of children's institutions. A local paper, which reported the program in 1929 under the headline "No More Oliver Twists," related that students were "drilled within an inch of their lives in psychology, psychiatry, essentials of medicine, immigration backgrounds, community resources and mental hygiene." Although this two-year program was dropped during the depression of the thirties, institutes on the administration of children's institutions were organized from time to time in later years.

Interest in the field of child welfare during the twenties coincided with the rising influence of psychiatry in the social work field. At Associated Charities, staff members returning from summer institutes and association meetings began to stimulate interest in incorporating these new insights into casework treatment. In 1920 Helen Hanchette of the agency reported,

Psychiatry . . . is giving us new light on our methods of dealing
with people. In the past our approach had been from the standpoint
of externals. In order to really bring about better adjustment in the
lives of our clients, it is necessary to understand the deep-seated
motives for human conduct. . . . After we learn more of the meaning
of people's attitudes of mind, the possibilities of more effective treatment by the casework method seem unlimited.[6]

During the same year a section of the Cleveland Foundation's
Hospital and Health Survey considered the community's facilities
for mental hygiene. Dr. Thomas Salmon, medical director of the
National Committee for Mental Hygiene and one of the participants in the Cleveland survey, was a national leader in the movement to secure expanded facilities for the study and treatment of
delinquents. At the 1920 annual meeting of Associated Charities
seven hundred people came to hear Dr. Salmon talk on "Mental
Handicaps and Family Welfare."

One year later, in 1921, Lakeside Hospital opened a Mental Hygiene Clinic, and the School of Applied Social Sciences announced
a course in psychiatric social work, which was financed by the Red
Cross and taught by Dr. George H. Reeve. Although Reeve was
appointed to the faculty of SASS, a training course in psychiatric
social work failed to materialize at this time because of "lack of
properly prepared applicants." In the school year 1922-23 Dr.
Reeve conducted three non-credit courses for staff workers—two
in Human Conduct and Its Disorders and one in Psychiatric Social Work—which drew a total of over 130 students.

The growing desire of social workers to learn the new psychiatric approach was further encouraged by the establishment of
the Child Guidance Clinic, which was opened in 1924 with the
financial support of the Commonwealth Fund. Since 1922 there
had been correspondence between SASS and the Commonwealth
Fund about the development of a psychiatric social work program, but it was the Mental Hygiene Council of the Welfare Federation that was responsible for establishing the Child Guidance
Clinic in Cleveland. The primary purpose of the new agency was
to furnish educational experiences and consultation services to the
community, but its first students of social work were from the
Smith College School of Social Work, which had been started in

1918 to teach psychiatric social work. In 1925 the director of the clinic, Dr. Lawson G. Lowry, opened its facilities to students at SASS for instruction and clinical demonstrations, and the following year he conducted a two-hour course on The Dynamics of Human Behavior. But despite increased psychiatric activity on both the local and national scenes it was 1928 before SASS opened a specialization in psychiatric social work, with the financial aid of the Commonwealth Fund.

The program that made the most promising start at the School of Applied Social Sciences during the early twenties was a course in group work, which was given impetus by the postwar interest in providing healthful leisure-time activities for children and young adults. The postwar years, which saw nativistic suspicion of the foreign-born and a fourfold increase in the Negro population of the city, brought community tensions which alarmed responsible elements in Cleveland.

In 1919 a Cleveland Foundation survey of recreational needs and resources in Cleveland focused attention on problems in this area. As a result of the survey's report, the Welfare Federation organized a Recreation Council composed of representatives of public and private agencies providing recreational services. The Recreation Council, in turn, began to implement the survey's strong recommendation for more and better trained recreation personnel by conducting training courses for settlement house workers and playground leaders.

This increased awareness of the need for trained workers outside the field of casework led to negotiations between SASS, the Cleveland Foundation, and the Cleveland Welfare Federation about establishing the Division of Play and Recreation, which had been proposed at the time of the School's inception. Although these plans never materialized, the seeds for a course in group work were already being planted by Mildred Chadsey in lectures on community organization that she gave in the 1921 Red Cross extension course. The following year she gave a full credit course at the School on Community Service or "Group Work."

Meanwhile, strong community support for group work education was being organized by Mrs. Albert H. Bates, president of the Cleveland Girls Council. On May 31, 1923, she addressed a gathering of prominent Clevelanders to secure support for such a program at the School of Applied Social Sciences. Mrs. Bates began by pointing out that until recently it was a generally accepted idea that anyone interested in young people would have the ability to be a good leader of children's groups, just as mothers were supposed to know instinctively the best way in which to bring up their children. Pointing to the current lack of discipline among young people, Mrs. Bates challenged such assumptions and asserted that mothers and leaders had failed because they lacked proper training. She called for knowledge of group psychology to prevent mobs and knowledge of child psychology to teach the individual to become a constructive member of the group. Mrs. Bates noted that the university had already recognized the need to train social workers dealing with individuals and families, and she urged her audience to support the establishment of a group-work course that would provide trained leaders, not only for the Cleveland Girls Council, but for many other agencies of the Welfare Federation.[7]

This superb speech encouraged a number of prominent Clevelanders to form an advisory committee and, more important, to pledge financial support to establish the nation's first university training course in group service at the School of Applied Social Sciences. Wilbur I. Newstetter, later director of the program, recalled that the impetus for professional training in group work came not only from the new education in social work with the underprivileged, but also from recognition that normal individuals could benefit from skillful leadership in adjustment to the group. Furthermore, caseworkers began to recognize the value of the group as a tool in the treatment process.

In the fall of 1923 eleven students were enrolled in the group service course, which was approved by the university on a three-year trial basis. Mildred Chadsey, who was appointed to the staff of SASS as director of the program, reported at the end of the first year that some problems were caused by the uneven educational and vocational backgrounds of the students.[8] Some agency workers who did not have college degrees were enrolled in the program because the agencies wanted them to have the educational experience. Some students with college degrees had had no previous experience in agencies. Miss Chadsey found that those with sound educational backgrounds did better in both classwork and field practice, and she anticipated that standards for admittance in the future could be raised to provide a more uniform group of students.

The group service course was designed to train workers in the principles and methods of dealing with groups through club and class leadership and through promotional activities and administrative work in social settlements, community centers, and young men's and women's organizations—all groups that tried to give direction to the lives of their members through the group association. A threefold program was established to achieve the aims of the course: (1) a minimum of three classroom hours a week in theories and principles, (2) a minimum of twelve hours in supervised field work with weekly conferences to evaluate the student's performance, and (3) courses of instruction in special skills such as public speaking, parliamentary procedure, methods of teaching English to foreigners, play production, storytelling, music and choral singing, and indoor and outdoor games for all age groups. In addition to this program several students engaged in special research projects related to the operation of their agencies. For example, two students studied the Negro problem and how it affected the work of a settlement that was called upon to serve an increasing Negro population, and others made a study of recreational and social agencies which served Negroes.

The focus of this program, which was taken by all students in their first year of study, was far more academic than the training classes held at Associated Charities. It is significant that the class in the theory and practice of group work was carefully separated from classes in the special skills that were considered important to group workers. For the first time the intellectual discipline of research projects was incorporated into the main body of study for interested and qualified students. In the past one of the stumbling blocks for social workers wanting to earn a master's degree had been the thesis requirement, which was difficult for casework students who were working full time in their agencies. Miss Chadsey noted in a report of the program after the first year that in the future they hoped to give more course content on the techniques of working with individuals in groups.

Students were placed at the Woodland Center, Hiram House, Girls Council, Phillis Wheatley Association, Superior Avenue Presbyterian Church, and the Council Educational Alliance; one student was employed in special club work. The number of hours of work and the student's financial arrangements varied with the individual field work. Although salaried students were necessarily held down to one job, arrangements were made for non-salaried students to receive a wide range of work experiences. Miss Chadsey realized at the end of the first year of the course that it was possible for the School to give more direction to students' work within the agencies, which had proved anxious to co-operate with such supervision.

The success of the one-year program in group service, and the enthusiastic response of the advisory committee and the agencies with which the faculty co-operated, encouraged the School to add another year of training to the group service program, which became a group work specialization equivalent to the casework specializations in family and child welfare.

But in 1925, eight years after its inception, the School of Applied Social Sciences, which had continued to operate on a precarious financial base, suddenly found itself faced by a threat to its very existence. Not only did the university begin to challenge the School's annual deficit, but it also questioned the whole concept of including social work education among the graduate schools of the university. The program provided for social workers had served as an excellent apprenticeship for the city's welfare agencies, but it had hardly begun to provide the intellectual breadth and depth essential to a new profession.

NOTES

1 William H. Baldwin to Charles F. Thwing, October 27, 1914.
2 William H. Baldwin to Charles F. Thwing, November 7, 1914.

[3] James F. Jackson to James E. Cutler, January 15, 1915.

[4] Quoted in Eleanor Farnham, *Pioneering in Public Health Nursing Education* (Cleveland: The Press of Western Reserve University, 1964), 37. This is an account of the University Public Health Nursing District, 1917-62, and the reader who wishes to know more about the public health program at SASS should consult this history.

[5] Waite, 156.

[6] *Ibid.*, 178.

[7] Speech by Mrs. Albert H. Bates, May 11, 1923.

[8] Miss Chadsey had been employed by Mayor Newton D. Baker a few years earlier as chief of the Bureau of Housing and Sanitation of the City of Cleveland. Before joining the faculty in 1917 she had been the executive secretary of the Consumers League of Ohio.

III.   Crisis and Response

Although the School of Applied Social Sciences had initiated
three new social work programs during the first eight years of its
existence, there were important areas of weakness within the curriculum. Furthermore, major problems of finance and university
recognition dominated the School during the early years. The resulting dissension was hidden from public view by what one faculty member later characterized as "glowing statements of purpose."

The School's financial resources, apart from the funds provided
for the Division of Public Health Nursing by the Welfare Federation and the city government, were limited to a small endowment,
occasional annual donations, and revenue from student fees. Frequent annual deficits had usually been met by the university,
which became increasingly dissatisfied with this obligation. In
1923 the School was able to cover its deficit by securing $7,500
from the Community Fund, but officials of this fund-raising organization pointed out that "maintenance of the school [was]
properly the University's responsibility." The following year the
university's request for further aid from the Community Fund was
ignored.

Crippled by lack of money, the School had not been able to
build an adequate faculty for its program. The major teaching responsibility at SASS was carried by faculty members attached to
social work agencies. The two casework courses and the group
service course were designed primarily to equip students with a
knowledge of the techniques of social work and the resources of
the community. In some instances students were required to take
other university courses to supplement their undergraduate backgrounds, and a few members of the university faculty and the
social work community gave occasional lectures in their areas of
specialty; but there was no real attempt to buttress the practical
work of the students with a comprehensive body of knowledge
from the relevant social sciences.

Dean Cutler retained the chairmanship of the sociology department and his teaching responsibilities outside of the School. Even
when he proposed a fivefold expansion of SASS in 1923, he continued to visualize the office of dean as a part-time position. Cutler
viewed his role at SASS as that of an administrative co-ordinator,
and he did not exert aggressive, imaginative leadership to develop
a program of social work education. He was, in fact, held in a vise
of pressing financial problems and short-range agency needs. He
believed that "advancement in the field of professional education
[was] conditioned by certain factors in community life," such as
the standards of professional service demanded in the community,
the amount the community was willing to pay for these services,
and the kind of education demanded by the students.[1]

Cutler was greatly influenced by James F. Jackson, the executive of Associated Charities whose training courses had been taken
over by the School. He and other agency executives were anxious
for the School to provide training for their workers, but they were
not willing to have their workers relinquish the time necessary to
achieve a broad professional education. As long as family and
child welfare students took the university casework course, the
agencies were prepared to employ them without a master's degree. When Cutler suggested increasing academic course-work
requirements, the attitude of the family and child welfare agencies was characterized by Jackson's response: "I know that this
degree business is right, and we want it, but don't forget that our
clients and our community are always our responsibility as well
as the development of our students."[2] Jackson was, after all, an
agency executive—not an educator.

But there was discontent among the students who had entered
what they had been told was a graduate professional school. By
1923 over forty-seven students had taken at least two years in the
Division of Family Welfare and Social Service, and not one of
them had been awarded a degree. Since 1920 the School's social
work personnel had pressed the university for a decision on the
granting of a master's degree. One of the basic problems was that
of evaluating the field work program in terms of University credit.
It was finally decided that college graduates who had taken a cer-

tain number of undergraduate courses in the social sciences would be admitted for a master's program that included the casework course and field work performed under the School's supervision. A thesis based on original research in the area of applied knowledge was required of all students. In June of 1924 Western Reserve University awarded a Master's in Social Administration to thirteen graduates of the School of Applied Social Sciences. But despite the university degree, Cleveland social workers attending national conferences found themselves chided about the apprenticeship program at SASS.[3]

The arrival of a new president at Western Reserve University in 1924 led to a fresh examination of the School's program and financial situation. Robert E. Vinson, who became president of the university three years after President Thwing retired, did not share his predecessor's commitment to the School of Applied Social Sciences. Vinson was brought to Reserve to preside over the expansion of the university's school of medicine, and he tended to cast a cold eye upon other university schools which did not operate on a sound financial base. Shortly after his inauguration he called upon Miss Sydnor Walker, a director of the Laura Spelman Rockefeller Memorial Foundation, to give him an evaluation of the School's educational program.

In May of 1925 Miss Walker sent President Vinson a memorandum describing the situation as she saw it. She wrote:

> In cooperation with the School, the Associated Charities, the Children's Bureau, the Humane Society, and the Girls' Council have arranged training courses for those joining their staffs. In the case of each of these organizations field work of students in training is supervised by a member of the school faculty, who is also a staff member of the organization. Thus, the connection between the theoretical and practical training of the student is unusually close, and the school is meeting the needs of these agencies very completely.

On the other hand, Miss Walker pointed out that other casework agencies such as the American Red Cross, the Jewish Social Service Bureau, and the Women's Protective Association were not able to secure training in their own agencies for their workers. She felt that the School's arrangement of offering the American Red

Cross and the Jewish Social Service staff members a two-hour course without credit was quite unsatisfactory. The three training agencies received funds from the Community Chest to provide stipends for students and to pay part of the salary of the students' field supervisors, but no such funds were available to subsidize such programs in other agencies.[4]

Noting that SASS was organized along "markedly different lines from the usual graduate school of a university," Miss Walker reported that students were not admitted to the School solely on the basis of their previous education and personal qualifications. Rather, they first had to be accepted as staff members by one of the agencies co-operating with the School, and during the two years of training the students had to do their field work in the organization which paid their salaries. "While the justification for this unusual arrangement . . . [was the claim that] . . . the student derives a maximum benefit in practical experience by becoming a member of a social organization," Miss Walker pointed out that the plan automatically limited the students who enrolled in the School to the number who could be absorbed into the working staff of the participating agencies and resulted in an insufficient number of trained workers to meet the needs of the Cleveland community.[5]

Miss Walker concluded that the present program of accepting applicants to the School according to the staff needs of certain local agencies was educationally unsound. She recommended to President Vinson that "if the School was to continue as a graduate school, it [was] desirable that it secure finances under independent control [to] enable it to provide instruction and field experience as best adapted to the needs of the student and the general requirements of the community for social workers."[6]

A month after this report was issued the university Board of Trustees passed a resolution holding the School of Applied Social Sciences responsible for its annual deficit. The board further warned that unless additional funds could be provided for the School, its work would have to be curtailed or modified in order to bring it within available income. When Vinson informed the SASS faculty of the trustees' decision, he offered them a slim hope for the future by recommending that they engage in a review of the School's policy with reference to the need for professional education of social workers and the specific function of SASS in this field. A faculty committee was assigned to undertake the task of self-examination.

Meanwhile, Cutler, who felt that Miss Walker's assessment suffered from "her unfamiliarity with certain local aspects of a very complex situation," began to mobilize support within the community and across the nation. President Vinson received letters supporting the School from prominent Clevelanders; and Jane Addams wrote from Hull House to tell Vinson that she shared regret "with social workers all over the country that there is a chance that your School of Applied Social Sciences may be closed." She continued:

> I always feel most strongly the need for professional training in social work, and that this training should be connected with Universities is important because it is most desirable that textbooks or at least source material should be gotten together as speedily as possible. Research is therefore quite as important as teaching field work, if our profession is to attain the standing which it deserves. Research of course cannot be secured unless the schools have University affiliation, and we hope very much that your Board will be able to reconsider its position.[7]

On November 18, 1925, the SASS Committee on Review of Policy presented a seventeen-page report to President Vinson.[8] It was the work of three faculty members—James F. Jackson, Director of the Division of Social Administration; Charles E. Gehlke, faculty member of the sociology department and instructor at SASS; and Mildred Chadsey, director of group service work. The report, "A Review of the Aims and Methods of the School of Applied Social Sciences," was a serious attempt to justify the operation of the School. After first addressing themselves to explaining the need for a graduate school for the professional education of social workers attached to Western Reserve University, the committee members went on to describe the plan of work at SASS and the outlook for the future.

The report made the point that the profession of social work grew out of the need to assist those people who were unable to cope with the complexities of a modern, industrial, urbanized society:

> Just as . . . [the society has] . . . trained engineers, chemists, bacteriologists, public health physicians, public health nurses, sanitary inspectors, to oversee the multitude of details pertaining to the physical well-being of a city's inhabitants, . . . [so the society] . . . must have similarly specialized professional workers to care for those classes in our population who are being ground between the upper millstone of the urban situation and the lower millstone of their own weaknesses and incapacity.

The committee described the profession of social work, which grew out of the complexities of modern society, as "an art based on scientifically ascertained facts." The School "combines the theory of the classroom with actual work in the field," which is carefully controlled in the interest of the students' education.

After describing the current areas of education offered at SASS, the report looked to future needs for programs in medical, psychiatric, and school social work, as well as casework education for those working in child correction agencies. The committee also noted the importance of doing more research and asserted that "the School of Applied Social Sciences only half fulfills the promise of its name if it does not engage in research."

A copy of the "Review" was mailed by Dean Cutler to a number of prominent Clevelanders who were active supporters of the community's welfare agencies. He enclosed a covering letter in which he made the following points:

> A conservative estimate from the figures of the Community Fund reveals upward of 150,000 different persons served annually by the privately supported welfare agencies of Cleveland. These agencies have an annual budget of nearly ten millions of dollars; they require this coming year nearly four and a half million dollars in contributions; they have property estimated by a leading Cleveland realtor to be worth twenty-five millions.
>
> The sole agency in Cleveland engaged in training executives for this tremendous community undertaking is our School of Applied Social Sciences. This School, and with it the source of supply of competent social work executives and social workers, is threatened with curtailment of its activities by reason of inadequate endowment—and this at a time when conservative expansion is urgently needed.[9]

Despite appeals from people such as Jane Addams and the persuasive "Review" presented by the SASS faculty, it is doubtful that the School would have survived had it not been for the momentum given to social work education by the group service program that had recently been developed. In 1924, the year the first master's degree was awarded to a student in group service, the Reverend Joel B. Hayden of Fairmount Presbyterian Church gave an address at the School's commencement dinner and commented on the development of the new course:

> It advances this conviction—that the task of practical democracy is to produce intelligent, tactful and practical social engineers who will meet *real situations in a real way* . . . equipped with all the knowledge and historic background that class instruction and discussion can give them. This means a *professional* standard.

Hayden went on to analyze professional education in terms of Alfred Whitehead's categories of learning. Essentially the School was a fusion of the accumulation of facts and the "training of affective and will centers for the job of living—the matter of adult experience."[10]

Hayden was to play an increasingly important part in the development of the group work program, which became one of the most important sections of the School and earned an international reputation. Hayden's brother-in-law, Wilbur I. Newstetter, was the director of Woodland Center, a settlement supported by the Presbytery of Cleveland and originally organized by the Woodland Avenue Presbyterian Church. Although the church moved when its parishioners left the area as Negroes began to come in, both Hayden and Newstetter were concerned about the rising antagonisms that occurred as a result of the population changes. They were anxious that the Center help to develop leadership within the Negro community, and, if possible, be run by Negroes.

At the same time there was increased awareness of the complete lack of recreational facilities in the whole southeastern section of Cleveland. Group service students at Woodland Center had joined other organizations in the area to study this part of the city and had come to the conclusion that the Polish and Slovenian people living there were in great need of social welfare assistance.

Newstetter was one of the community leaders in a movement to establish a new community center in this section of the city. Out of his relationship with the School of Applied Social Sciences came the idea of using the proposed new center and the Woodland Center as the nucleus of a neighborhood teaching unit for the group service course.

In February of 1926, when Dean Cutler approached the Welfare Federation to secure support for a group service training center, he noted that SASS already had a model for the proposal in the University Public Health Nursing District. Since the School's enrollment was limited by the number of remunerative field placements available, a social agency conceived primarily as a place of training would be of great advantage to the university. Commenting that social work education had suffered in the past from early specialization, he observed that the trend was changing to give students training primarily as social workers, while allowing them to specialize enough to be of remunerative value in their field work. Furthermore, one of the purposes of the project would be to attract men, who would be given a broad education in social work so that they could be considered for executive positions in the social welfare field. The project would be staffed by students and faculty members from SASS; and instead of building a settlement house in one location the School would rent houses at strategic points in the neighborhood so that resident workers would have close contact with people in the area.[11]

The Welfare Federation approved the university training center but could offer nothing but moral support for the project. Nevertheless, Hayden and Newstetter moved ahead to explore securing financial support from the Laura Spelman Rockefeller Memorial Foundation and the Community Chest; but they found that the lack of confidence in the School which had been expressed in the trustees' resolution of June, 1925, was inhibiting their proposal. The citizen advisory committee which supported the group service training course met with a committee that was promoting the idea of a new settlement house in the southeast section of Cleveland. Out of this meeting came a statement calling the attention of university officials to the "stigma" that had been placed on

SASS by the June resolution. The committees pointed out that the resolution could not fail to affect the decision of any foundation or individual who was approached for funds, and they recommended that the trustees of the university rescind the resolution and endorse the work already accomplished by the School. The Board of Trustees of Western Reserve University did rescind the SASS resolution on May 14, 1926.

Meanwhile, Hayden used his influence in the community to gather financial support for the proposed university extension program. By May 27, 1926, he was able to write to Cutler that he had secured $55,000 for the first year's operation of the new program, but he also requested that the university's Board of Trustees assume the School's $5,000 deficit for the current year of operation. Hayden added that he and Newstetter were meeting that night with "some of the strongest laymen of Fairmount Church" to place before them "as Christian citizens of Cleveland their opportunity . . . in promoting the best interest of social and religious idealism in the city of Cleveland."[12]

The influence of this financial support,* the strong backing of influential members of the community, and indications that the Laura Spelman Rockefeller Memorial Foundation was interested in assisting the expansion of the School produced immediate results. The university trustees voted to contribute $5,000 to the budget of SASS, and President Vinson announced publicly that he considered the School of Applied Social Sciences to be "one of the greatest assets to the University, second only to the medical school." The following year the Rockefeller Foundation gave a five-year matching-fund grant to the School. By 1932, when this grant was terminated, the School had received $117,000 from the fund and the university had contributed $107,500.

In the short run the vigorous efforts of those associated with the group service course saved the social work program of the School

---

* While various members of the Advisory Committee to the Group Service Division gave financial support, the University Neighborhood Centers were largely supported by Mrs. Dudley S. Blossom. From 1926 to 1941, when the School severed all connection with the program, this good citizen of Cleveland gave over $360,000 to support these pioneers in social work.

from collapse; in the long run the impact upon social work education in Cleveland was even more important. Those who joined together in the development of the group service program created an intellectual excitement that had not before been present in the Division of Social Administration; and increased financial support of the School not only provided for an expansion of its program, but also began to liberate it from the agency apprenticeships that had dominated its educational program for the previous ten years.

The Rockefeller funds were given not just to support the group service course, but to advance the entire program of social work education at the School. The subsequent expansion of SASS led to important organizational changes. For the first time in its history the School secured an adequate administrative staff. The appointment of Margaret Johnson as executive secretary and instructor in social administration marked the beginning of her long and fruitful service to SASS. The School also secured a registrar, a librarian, and three office secretaries; and additional office and classroom space was provided on the main campus of Western Reserve University. Increased financial resources allowed the School to bring in additional full-time faculty members and to employ many part-time instructors from other schools within the university.

When the School applied to the Rockefeller Foundation for funds, one of the projected areas of expansion was the field of medical social work. There had been considerable interest in this specialization at the School since 1920 when the Cleveland Hospital and Health Survey reported:

> It is curious that a community so advanced as is Cleveland in many respects should have made only a slight development in the social service activities of the hospitals and dispensaries.

There had been a social service department at Lakeside Hospital since 1913, and departments were opened at Mount Sinai Hospital in 1917 and at St. Vincent's Charity Hospital in 1919; but the survey noted that "in no department does there seem to be a clear recognition that the prime basis of social service in a hospital . . . is the assistance of medical treatment."[13]

When Lakeside Hospital reorganized its social service department to meet the criticisms of the survey, the director of the department expressed interest in the development of a training course in medical social work at SASS. Dean Cutler, who was interested in the field, took part in the American Hospital Association's study of education for medical social workers in 1922. In the early twenties the School attempted to provide medical information to students and caseworkers in various agencies, but no funds were available to open a new field of specialization.

In 1927, after the School's financial base was strengthened, Miss Agnes Schroeder was appointed to establish a course in medical social work. Miss Schroeder, a home economist who had received a year of training in the School's Family Welfare Division, was employed as a home economist at Associated Charities until 1921 when she joined the social service department at Lakeside Hospital. The educational program that was developed for medical social workers was planned in close collaboration with the American Association of Hospital Social Workers, and the Association's educational secretary, Miss Kate McMahon, came to Cleveland to help Miss Schroeder set up the course. Aside from courses in social work, medicine, and psychiatry, the curriculum of the medical social workers included courses such as Social Aspects of Disease, Nutrition and Dietotherapy, and Statistical Methods Applied to Medical Social Work. During the first semester of their education the medical social-work students were placed as a group in a district office of the Associated Charities to learn under supervision the casework approach to the study and treatment of human problems. During the second semester, field placement was in a hospital setting, and arrangements were made for the students to have a three-week placement in the Child Guidance Clinic during the summer before they completed their course, with five more weeks in a hospital setting. The course lasted for one academic year plus eight weeks, until 1931 when it became a two-year program.[14] Attempts were made to provide field placements in a number of hospitals in the community, but even as late as the 1940's some hospital administrators believed that social service work could be performed better by nurses with social work training.

A unique aspect of the program in medical social work was the School's decision to provide scholarships for students in this course instead of depending on remunerative field placements. The School formed an advisory committee of Clevelanders interested in this field of social work. Throughout the years the committee played an important role, not only in initiating the program and securing scholarships for qualified students, but also in securing acceptance of medical social work in the medical field.

In 1927 the expanded program of the School brought the appointment of the first psychiatric social worker as a full-time member of the faculty. Since the early 1920's the School had added an increasing number of courses dealing with the psychology and pathology of human behavior, but a program in psychiatric social work was slow in developing. It was Dean Cutler who remarked in 1928 that "it remained for the Commonwealth Fund to put on a demonstration clinic in Cleveland" before the School moved ahead. In 1928 SASS offered its first program in psychiatric social work—an advanced course which was limited until 1935 to students who had completed casework training. Students took six hours weekly in advanced courses such as Analytic Psychology, An Interpretation of Mental Testing, Psychology of the Abnormal, and Seminar in Psychiatric Case Work. Field work was performed in two agencies—the Child Guidance Clinic for nine months, and the adult section of Mt. Sinai Hospital's Mental Hygiene Clinic for three months. In the first year of the program students who had been selected to take the course received one hundred dollars a month from the agencies in which they were placed, but the following year the Commonwealth Fund initiated a plan of providing eight scholarships each year. In 1929 Anna Belle Tracy, who had been closely connected with the School in her position as executive secretary of the local Home Service Section of the American Red Cross, was appointed to the faculty to direct the psychiatric social work course.

Not only were new programs added to the Division of Social Administration, but there were also changes in the programs which had already been established. The first step in broadening the base of family casework, along the lines of the suggestions which had been made by Sydnor Walker, was the inclusion of the Jewish Social Service and the local chapter of the American Red Cross (Home Section) as co-operating agencies in the family casework course. As a result of this change the instructors in that course left their quarters in the Associated Charities' offices to establish their own office and classrooms (in the same building) downtown. In 1931 space was provided for family casework classrooms and offices on the main campus of the university.

Another move which tended to separate the student from his role as an "employee" of the field placement agency was the faculty's decision to require that students, rather than the agency in which they worked, be responsible for paying their own tuition. By 1928 the School was also able to persuade field placement agencies to establish a uniform salary schedule for students. The School continued to make provision for a minimum schedule of supervised field work for students who could afford to pursue their studies without financial aid.

In 1928, as the number of family casework students requiring field placement increased, the Associated Charities initiated an experimental program in field placement under the direction of Marjorie Boggs, an agency supervisor who had received a master's degree from SASS in 1924. Under this plan six students, who wished to have more time to take elective courses and to work more intensively with smaller case loads, were placed in the Buckeye office of Associated Charities. During the nine months of the experiment the students worked in the field just three days a week and received only half of the customary student stipend, but they had the educational advantage of being supervised by a field instructor who carried no agency responsibilities and was free to devote her entire time to the student's educational needs. Furthermore, the student was free to spend more time reading and studying as well as taking additional classroom work. Two results of the experiment were the development of sound educational criteria for the selection of cases for first-year students and the improvement of methods of student supervision, including the use of the group conference as an educational tool.[15]

At the end of the nine-month period the students returned to the regular second-year casework program. Although those who participated in the experiment praised its value to both students and agency, the plan was never extended beyond the Buckeye office of Associated Charities. In 1931 the program fell victim to the financial crisis that was brought on by the Depression.

There were also important curriculum changes that occurred subsequent to the School's period of crisis in 1925. Formerly the catalogue of SASS had stated that a student who satisfied the admission requirements, completed sixty hours of work, and presented a thesis would receive a Master of Science in Social Administration. The "work" required was not clearly spelled out, and the catalogue further stated that "the results of the work done, rather than the time spent, determine the amount of credit." In the 1927-28 catalogue requirements for a degree were more specifically defined: a minimum of 15 semester hours of classroom work, a minimum of 15 semester hours of supervised field work (three hours weekly of field work were considered equivalent to one semester hour), and a master's thesis.

Furthermore, education for mutually exclusive specializations within social work began to lessen as more educational emphasis was placed on a common core of knowledge. All caseworkers took a number of courses in common, including Introduction to Social Work, Essentials of Medicine for Social Workers, Motivation of Human Behavior, and Social Psychiatry—Adult. In the second year of their education students in family casework and child welfare took more common courses: Social Psychiatry—Childhood, Case Discussion of Social-Psychiatric Problems—Adult and Childhood, Administration of Social Agencies, Community Organization, and Case Analysis. The group service students shared the courses entitled Introduction to Social Work, Administration of Social Agencies, and Community Organization. They also took Introduction to Social Casework and Dynamics of Human Behavior—courses which were very similar in content to those given to the casework students. Instructors for these courses included doctors from the medical school and the psychiatrist who directed the Child Guidance Clinic, as well as members of the SASS faculty.

The enlargement in the group service course that occurred in 1927 brought in new faculty members who were not bound by the traditions that surrounded the School or the patterns of thought that had dominated social workers in Cleveland. Henry Miller Busch, Thornton Merriam, Clara A. Kaiser, and Estelle Bonnell came with a variety of educational and vocational experiences that enriched the education of the group service students. The creation of the University Neighborhood Centers as a teaching laboratory enabled the group service faculty to experiment with educational programs to meet the needs of the students and the community they were to serve when they graduated.

The group work* faculty gave considerable thought to the educational experience that they wished to give their students in order to equip them to be social workers. They sought to reconcile "the rival demands of 'production' and 'good education'" by including the executives of agencies in the discussion of curriculum development. Such inclusion allowed the executives to share in planning the educational experience, but precluded domination by these executives in terms of short-term needs of the agencies. The faculty of the group work course recognized that "students needed additional theoretical groundwork in related basic sciences . . . if they were to be ready for the responsible positions for which they were being prepared."[16]

The changing pattern of social work education was evident at a meeting of group work faculty and agency executives who considered the need for students to have a course in the philosophy of social work. Newstetter reported that a faculty committee had discussed such a course for second-year students and had come to the conclusion that it should be offered in the form of an institute so that practicing social workers as well as students could attend. He proposed that educators and social workers such as John Dewey, Hastings H. Hart, and Florence Kelley could be invited to speak in order to stimulate real thinking regarding the aims and purposes of social work. One agency executive inquired if the

---

* The term "group work" was substituted for group service in 1929 because the faculty felt that this term had become the one generally used in the social work profession.

real basis for social work were an acceptance of the present social order, and thus largely palliative, or whether social work were to undertake building the foundations of a more just and ideal order of society. Those attending the meeting agreed that it was desirable for social workers to question some of the fundamental principles involved in social living, and they doubted that the majority of students graduating from SASS had such ability. Such thinking was in sharp contrast to the philosophy that the social worker's role was "to adjust man to his environment."[17]

NOTES

[1] James E. Cutler, "Address to the American Association of Hospital Social Workers," Cleveland, May 29, 1926.

[2] Marion Cook McGowan to James E. Cutler, June 9, 1941. Mrs. McGowan was a director of training in casework with families during the early years of SASS.

[3] "List of Graduates from the Course in Family Case Work since the Associated Charities entered the School of Applied Social Sciences," prepared for Mr. Rowland Haynes, Welfare Federation, October 31, 1923; Waite, 210-11.

[4] Sydnor H. Walker, "Memorandum: School of Applied Social Sciences of Western Reserve University," May 9, 1925.

[5] *Ibid.*

[6] *Ibid.*

[7] Jane Addams to Dr. Robert Vinson, October 2, 1925.

[8] Mildred Chadsey, C. E. Gehlke (chairman), and James F. Jackson, "A Review of the Aims and Methods of the School of Applied Social Sciences: Presented to the Faculty by its Committee on Review of Policy," November 18, 1925.

[9] James E. Cutler to members of Advisory Committees of SASS, December, 1925.

[10] Joel B. Hayden, "The Need for People Who Know and Can and Do" (talk at Annual Dinner of SASS), June 9, 1924.

[11] James E. Cutler, "Outline of Plans for University Center," February 9, 1926.

[12] Joel B. Hayden to James E. Cutler, May 27, 1926.

[13] Quoted in James E. Cutler *et al.*, "Memorandum on the Requirements and Curriculum for Medical Social Work" (mimeographed), January 19, 1934, 18.

[14] *Ibid.*, 19-24.

[15] Waite, 213-15.

[16] Thornton Merriam, "Memorandum on the Major Problems which give Us Concern," December, 1927.

[17] The Consulting Staff of the Group Service Division, "Minutes," February 9, 1928.

IV.   Defining a Professional Education

The group workers' eagerness to examine the role of the profession of social work in relation to the society of which it was a part was a product of traditional settlement-house involvement in social reform. In Cleveland during the progressive era Goodrich House had provided the catalyst for the formation of the Consumers League and the Legal Aid Society—organizations which actively lobbied for legislation that would remedy some of the hardships faced by the "clients" of the settlement houses. From the group of volunteers attached to Goodrich House had come many of the men who pressed for progressive reforms at the local and state levels of government.

To some extent a concern with the broad social problems of the community became a part of the new profession of group work, but group workers were also influenced by strong forces that were already well established within the field of social work. The emphasis on the importance of developing scientifically based techniques for helping people provided the impetus for group workers to concentrate on helping the individual through the structure of interpersonal group relationships. Roy Lubove points out that the social workers' preoccupation with developing a distinctive technique or method was a part of their strong desire to establish a professional identity—a goal which made them shy away from social action.[1]

Dean Cutler, who remained in office until 1940, was convinced that social workers should not become crusaders for social legislation. When the School was still determining its role in the community, he told students:

> The role of the militant reformer and agitator is not a formula for a profession . . . The detached viewpoint gives balance, poise and judgment—all of which bring confidence from givers and supporters and from patients and beneficiaries. No professional man or woman can succeed without winning the confidence of a constituency.[2]

James F. Jackson of Associated Charities, who had set the stage for professional social work in Cleveland by making a distinction between the trained worker and the volunteer, was also careful not to involve his agency in social action. Although he recognized "adverse conditions that threatened health, happiness and self-support," he believed:

> The Associated Charities could not pour a large stream of energy into general undertakings and at the same time meet its unmistakable responsibility for the development and improvement of service to individual families and for leadership in the promotion of cooperation among social agencies.[3]

Jackson preferred to bear witness to social conditions which needed correction through the strong connections that he and various board members had with the Chamber of Commerce, which had its own productive social action committees during the progressive era.

By the late 1920's the profession of social work was already putting down roots in a psychiatric explanation of human behavior, which turned the social workers' attention further away from the environmental conditions which so often brought their clients to them. The "Freudian plant" was so firmly rooted that not even the storms of the Depression were able to dislodge it. Not only did the School of Applied Social Sciences add more courses related to psychiatry, but it also invited special lecturers to discuss the new field with students and agency staff members. The leader of one of the institutes sponsored by the School in 1929 was Virginia Robinson, associate director of the Pennsylvania School of Social Work. An evangelist in promoting the psychiatric point of view among social workers, she wrote that

> all social case work, in so far as it is thorough and in so far as it is good case work, is mental hygiene. Case work not founded on the point of view of personality and adjustment for which mental hygiene contends is simply poor case work, superficial in diagnosis and blind in treatment.[4]

When she led the institute in Cleveland she asserted that "the relationship between the worker and client was the significant element in treatment." A worker from Associated Charities who attended the institute later wrote that "as Miss Robinson used the term 'relationship', it seemed to take on almost a mystical connotation—something to be striven for, but could . . . [it] . . . ever be attained by ordinary mortals?"[5] As such psychiatric concepts were incorporated into casework methodology, they provided a substantial underpinning for the School's assertion that social work was a profession based on scientific knowledge and technique, and assisted in differentiating the trained worker from the one without training.

As caseworkers became more and more "absorbed in function and technique as these related to the individual problem,"[6] those who established the group service program were motivated by a combination of Christian idealism and progressive educational philosophy to use group work agencies to develop social cohesiveness and democratic participation within immigrant neighborhoods. Operating in a city that was dominated by nationality enclaves and working with individuals as well as groups within these communities, group workers tried to help their clients meet the many problems they faced—adjustment to a new country, racial conflict, tensions between the foreign-born and their Americanized children, and the marginal incomes and unemployment that plagued them during the Depression.

The most significant part of the early group service program was the University Neighborhood Centers, which became a part of the School in 1926. Wilbur I. Newstetter, who was appointed director of the UNC, became the dominant figure in the group service course. By 1928 the UNC was in full operation, with four rented houses in different parts of the district providing living quarters for resident students and faculty members. Operating on the assumption that the best way to help people in this area was to assist them to develop their own resources and leadership capacities, faculty members and students did not try to use the houses as settlements (except insofar as they lived in the neighborhoods), but rather tried to use existing facilities such as neighborhood schools and libraries for community centers and recreational areas. Project leaders hoped that by helping to organize members of the community to take action on their own behalf, local leadership would be stimulated to continue the work after the group workers had left. Thus they relied heavily on volunteers who were indigenous to the community.

Concomitant goals of the University Neighborhood Centers included both the training of students in such community organization and "built-in" research to establish a theoretical base for the group work process. The students selected for field practice in the UNC took the same course work as other group work students; but whereas those placed in more traditional settlements were limited to leading activity and discussion groups for children and adults, the UNC students found themselves conducting surveys, organizing clubs, and developing leadership for these clubs. A wide variety of community activities were carried out by the UNC staff, which organized a children's music school and a theater group, supervised summer street play and noontime playground activity at parochial schools, instigated the organization of a neighborhood athletic association—financed and staffed by the Cleveland School Board (this connection later led to a one-year field work placement in the Community Centers Department of the Board of Education), organized a very successful South-End Mutual Exchange for barter in the height of the Depression, and established overnight and residential camping for children in the neighborhood. An important project carried out by the faculty and the group-work advisory committee was the organization of a district council composed of leading figures in the neighborhood community.

Despite the service orientation of the UNC the faculty was careful to maintain sufficient flexibility to provide for experimental educational training and research. Noting that there were "few scientific generalizations about the group and how to manipulate it for educational character-building ends," Newstetter appointed Clara Kaiser as director of research. To study the group process Miss Kaiser supervised a program of keeping records of groups, both for administrative purposes and as an educational tool to provide a supplementary source of supervision and field instruction. The records, in which staff members attempted to describe the important factors in relation to the organization and development of each group, reflected social work's growing conviction of the importance of recognizing the worker's role in a professional relationship. Miss Kaiser observed:

> [The recorder] must see himself and his relationship to the group as well as that of other members. There is no evidence to support the premise that the subjective elements of the record are not vitally important in understanding the processes inherent in group life. Our experience has led to the belief that the recorder should recognize the difference between the subjective interpretation and the objective observation of group phenomena and that the former should be made with the narrative account of group activity as its basis.[7]

By the time the economic pressures of the Depression terminated the UNC project in 1936,* it had provided an important educational experience for over one hundred students and had stimulated several pieces of original research and publication on the social process in small groups. Grace Coyle, who came to SASS to be director of research at UNC in 1934, had already established a national reputation with the publication of her dissertation, *Social Process in Organized Groups*. Three years later her experience at UNC provided material for *Studies in Group Behavior*, in which she edited group records written by students under faculty supervision.

Many of those who taught and received their education at the University Neighborhood Centers played a significant role in developing group work and in establishing programs for group work education throughout the nation. In 1938 Newstetter left SASS to become chairman of the reorganized school of social work at the University of Pittsburgh. Grace Coyle, who replaced him as director of group work, continued to provide national and international leadership in the field of group work with her superb teaching and seminal publications.[8]

The University Neighborhood Center fulfilled the original goal of stimulating the programs that were needed in the neighborhood; and, to some extent, it was able to leave behind indigenous leaders who played an important role in the University Settle-

---

* The School continued to have a special teaching relationship with the new University Center which was established at this time, but this was completely terminated when the Welfare Federation took over the entire financing of the Center in the early 1940's.

ment, which replaced the UNC at the request of people in the neighborhood when the School was forced to leave. Only the severe financial limitations of the Depression prevented the School from establishing another such teaching center during the 1930's.

Thirty years later the School, under Dean Herman Stein, was able to secure both local and national support for the development of the Garden Valley Neighborhood House Training Center, as a "teaching center whose professional direction [would] be under the auspices of the School of Applied Social Sciences to enhance learning opportunities in child welfare for social work students." While the 1966 program contained interesting similarities to the UNC teaching-district experiment—the social agency for which the School assumed operating direction was the successor to Newstetter's pioneering Woodland Center and the area was, in the language of the past, a most needy community—there were also important differences. The fact that the community to be served was predominantly low-income Negro, rather than foreign-born immigrant, reflected important societal changes which had occurred in the intervening years. Plans for integrating the social work specializations (case work, group work, and community organization) and for co-ordinating various governmental services (for health, housing, education, welfare, and juvenile delinquency) demonstrated major advances in the profession of social work and in the field of government welfare. Most important of all was the fact that the Garden Valley project was proposed to take *preventative* action in a socially critical area that contained large numbers of young children.

During the 1920's the group service course also extended its educational program to training and research centers in summer camps. In 1925 a summer camp institute was conducted at the YWCA camp at Madison, Ohio. In addition to group work students from SASS, sixty-two counsellors and directors from camps conducted by social agencies in northern Ohio were present for three days of lectures, discussions, and demonstrations concerning summer camping. For a number of years thereafter the School sponsored summer camp institutes which the group work students were usually required to attend.

In 1926 Newstetter, who was also the director of the Presbyterian-sponsored Harkness Summer Camp, used the Harkness facilities to initiate what was known as the Wawokiye Camp Experiment. That year fifty-one disturbed and/or delinquent boys became part of a camping experience which was designed to help them with their problems. Although the experiment was not given university recognition until 1929, the program sponsored research in group work from the beginning. In the early years the staff of this camp included a psychiatrist and a psychologist from the Child Guidance Clinic and Ph.D. candidates from Columbia University who used research material from the experiment for their dissertations. Starting in 1929 group work students from SASS replaced the Columbia students.

Wawokiye Camp provided:

> A controlled experiment for developing techniques of observation and studying the processes of group adjustment. Data collected [included] ratings by the counsellors of the boys' adjustment to a tent group and to the camp as a whole; ratings by the boys of the desirability of certain companions in given situations; records made by counsellors of objective behavior and overt attitudes; tests of several types such as intelligence, medical examination, psychoneurotic inventory, and developmental age.[9]

In 1930 Newstetter and Marc J. Feldstein published *Wawokiye Camp: A Research Project in Group Work*. This was followed in 1938 by what most authorities regard as the first sociometric study, *Group Adjustment: A Study in Experimental Sociology* by Newstetter, Feldstein, and Theodore M. Newcomb, a social psychologist from Columbia.

The Depression, which brought a premature end to the exciting new programs of the Group Work Division, also curtailed plans for major revisions in the curriculum and field placement program of the casework sections. In the late 1920's the casework sections shared in the School's increased financial prosperity, but in the 1930's new ideas of offering clients intensive casework treatment gave way to the pressing need to hand out grocery orders or little doles of cash.

The School's largest placement agency, Associated Charities, was also the city's major relief agency. In 1922 Cleveland's economy-minded mayor, Fred Kohler, had dispensed with the city's relief department and turned its function over to Associated Charities. It was ironic that the agency that had requested this change for so long soon found itself deploring that "the necessary emphasis on relief administration tended to make workers 'relief-minded' and to dull their appreciation of other aspects of family problems." The task was fairly manageable during the 1920's, but even by 1929 the relief budget had risen to more than $600,000.[10]

In the closing months of that year the number needing relief doubled each month, with the result that the year ended with 2,980 families on the AC lists. At the height of the Depression in 1933, 177,969 of the county's male citizens were unemployed. To handle rapidly rising case loads, the Associated Charities hired untrained workers, who were designated "aides," and with the co-operation of SASS began an intensive recruiting program for the coming school year. Fourteen casework students entered a midyear class in February, 1930, and the following fall witnessed the largest enrollment in the School's history to that date. By July of 1933 there were 36,000 families registered with AC. The agency's staff rose from 184 full-time workers and 77 casework students in October, 1930, to a staff of 1,167 in the summer of 1933. While the SASS student body increased rapidly during the same period, it reached a peak of 265 students in the fall of 1934, and the number of students began to decrease after that year.[11]

At the same time Western Reserve University faced serious financial problems. By 1938 the university's indebtedness was two million dollars, and its income from endowment funds had fallen sharply. The School of Applied Social Sciences faced a comparable situation; the income from its small endowment fell from $20,000 in 1929 to $13,000 in 1938, while the amount received from gifts and grants-in-aid fell off even more. In 1932 the whole program of the School was in serious trouble, and only the Reverend Joel B. Hayden's vigorous pleading before the Rockefeller Foundation saved it from economic disaster. That summer the foundation presented the School with an outright gift of $82,000 to be paid out over a number of years. The University imposed cuts ranging from 15 to 25 per cent in faculty salaries and established a policy of refusing to hire any new faculty members, even to fill vacancies that might occur. During the 1930's the School of Applied Social Sciences not only lost faculty, but also lost some of the time of other faculty members, who worked part-time for agencies in the city.

The total situation placed a severe strain on both faculty and students at the School. The increased enrollment produced greatly increased teaching loads for the faculty; and the heavy case loads at the agencies were inevitably passed on to the students, allowing less time for field supervision and study. Many of the second-year students found themselves supervising aides, which led to a demand for new courses to help them handle such responsibilities. During the 1930's faculty members had to prepare and offer a whole collection of new courses related to major changes in the field of social welfare. Although the School decided against establishing a division of public welfare, by 1937 the curriculum included such courses as The State and Social Work, Industrial Problems, Social Security, Social Legislation, Public Welfare, Public Social Work in a Case Work Agency, and Financial Planning in Case Work.

The relationship between aides and professional social workers resulted in considerable controversy. Many of the former resented the fact that advancement within the agency was confined to those who had received graduate education. Some members of the community were highly critical of a program that enabled students to be paid for their educational experience. The whole situation was intensified when the Cuyahoga County Relief Administration was created in the summer of 1933. Of the 1,070 staff members who transferred from Associated Charities and the smaller number who came from the Jewish Social Service Bureau, the great majority of those who had direct contact with clients were untrained workers.

The problem of how to fit the aide into the field of social work was one that deeply concerned faculty members at SASS. Many of the aides had college degrees, had had previous experience in other professions such as teaching, and had taken some of the

School's staff workers' extension courses; but caseworkers who had struggled to achieve professional status were decidedly adverse to giving the old apprenticeship method of training a new birth of life. On the other hand, the impact of the Depression on the total society had reawakened social workers to the "outer needs" of people in distress, and it was obvious that the nation's schools of social work could not possibly supply a sufficient number of professional workers to staff the traditional casework agencies. As the "temporary emergency" became the Great Depression, the School of Applied Social Sciences began to consider staff workers courses to provide some of the basic knowledge and skills for untrained workers.

In 1933 Florence Day informed the general meeting of the School's faculty that the Family Division favored two steps: (1) an advanced course to be offered to supervisors of aides; (2) a general lecture course for aides consisting of ten or twelve lectures for which a fee would be charged but no credit granted toward a degree. The faculty agreed to the plan as an emergency measure which was not to shortcut education for the profession of social work.[12] But the approach was obviously unsatisfactory to aides. At a time when salaries were low, there was little incentive to spend money for a lecture course that would produce neither an increase in salary nor credit toward an advanced degree. When the matter came up for discussion a year later, the School adopted a proposal:

> At such times and in whatever sequence may be practicable [that there be offered] to salaried staff workers in Cleveland social agencies, who are graduates of accredited colleges, the following six courses, with the understanding that the offering of these courses carries no commitment beyond [graduate] credit for work satisfactorily completed:
> 1. Understanding of Human Behavior
> 2. Medical Information for Social Workers
> 3. Nationality and Racial Backgrounds
> 4. Administration of Unemployment Relief
> 5. Public Welfare Administration
> 6. Social Work and the Law[13]

In 1936 the experiences of the Depression stimulated a group of casework graduates to organize a series of round-table discussions to consider the education which they had received at SASS. Forty-two caseworkers met at a local restaurant for the first dinner-discussion meeting, at which a recent graduate presented a critique of the School's curriculum in light of social workers' current experiences in the field. He began by pointing out that in local public agencies and across the nation the scarcity of trained workers and the rapid development of federal programs had resulted in many trained workers' being placed in administrative positions; yet the casework courses at SASS had in no way prepared students for responsibilities in supervision and administration.[14]

The second point made in the paper was that "careful examination of the curriculum and faculty" indicated that the School failed to live up to the function which was implied in its name— The School of Applied Social Sciences. The graduate believed that the School should identify "more closely with active and pioneering scientists in the fields of psychology, economics and sociology," but his greatest emphasis was placed on the need for practical research in the practice of casework. He pointed to five areas for study and research:

1) Techniques for objectively evaluating the results of case work
2) development of methods of case recording which are more efficient, uniform, and readable
3) the classification and description of some of the most common types of cases found in the practice of social case work with a similar classification and description of the treatment steps employed in the case work
4) development of objective techniques for measuring environment and personality
5) collection of thousands of case records illustrating various types of cases, skillful case work diagnosis and successful treatment.[15]

The speaker acknowledged that these were ambitious projects, but he asserted that the profession could not hope to place itself on a scientific basis until the schools of social work and the agencies co-operated to establish well-financed research programs staffed by competent persons with casework and research training. Pointing out that the resulting establishment of a scientific basis for casework would be of great importance in educating the community to the competency of the profession, the speaker went on to assert that until caseworkers engaged in private practice to serve the economically self-sufficient, they could not consider themselves on a sound professional basis.[16]

The SASS graduate felt that his "biggest bone to pick with the School" was its lack of emphasis on social reform and social action. He said:

> We who have been face to face with problems confronting social work today have been struck by the dual role of social work: that of 'adjustments individual by individual between man and his social environment' and that of adjusting a hopelessly maladjusted social environment to meet the needs of large masses of individuals.[17]

Asserting that the School had failed to educate the students to social problems and the techniques of achieving social action, he suggested that students be given a required course in methods of social action.

The paper produced vigorous discussion and general agreement that social casework training was "too limited to individualized case work." It was suggested that in addition to a course on social issues and action, caseworkers might be given more of the material in the group work curriculum. There was also criticism of the inadequacy of the staff workers' course in supervision. With regard to research, those attending the meeting felt that the system of thesis writing then in effect was "too inflexible . . . to be of any real contribution to the advancement of professional social work."[18]

Minutes from this meeting of SASS casework graduates were received with considerable interest by the faculty of the School, which had been engaged in a constant attempt to evaluate its program and methods ever since the School's expansion in 1927. After consulting an expert in job analysis, the faculty decided in 1929 that there was need for an intensive study of the entire program of the School, but the projected cost of the study was $85,000, and by the 1930's money could not be found for such an "unproductive" project. Although the serious problems produced by the financial crisis of the period produced a series of faculty meetings, no important changes were made in the School's program. Many faculty members believed that if Dean Cutler could be persuaded to devote full time to his position at SASS, the School would be in a stronger financial and administrative position; but the dean was reluctant to give up the chairmanship of the sociology department and his teaching responsibilities within the university. Finally, as a result of faculty dissension and the diplomatic pressure of the university's president, Winfred G. Leutner, Cutler became the School's full-time dean in 1936.

By the middle thirties the School began to consider other administrative changes. A two-year experiment with a more unified division of casework was begun in 1937 as a result of the development during the previous year of a basic casework course, which was taken by all students in the specializations of family casework, child welfare, and medical social work. Preparing the course brought the casework faculty into closer contact and led to an attempt to unify the program further. During the experiment one faculty member was designated chairman of the combined casework division, with responsibility for co-ordinating the development of the basic casework course. This was a small move toward unity, for the specializations not only retained their own directors, who had to be consulted with reference to the basic course, but also retained complete responsibility for the remainder of their curriculum; for arrangements related to their field work placements; and for the selection, advising, and dismissal of their students.[19]

The struggle of generic versus specialized education was clearly indicated in 1938 during a faculty discussion about a proposed new casework program in home economics and nutrition work. The new program was approved by the policy committee of SASS over the strong objection of Newstetter. Acknowledging that there were constant pressures on schools of social work to develop various specializations, he argued:

> The main responsibility of the schools is to keep alive and effective the main portions of our curriculum—to build on the central trunk of the tree—so that we are sure we are including the fundamental courses for the larger field for which we are offering training.

> We must preserve one professional degree which will represent professional social work, otherwise we retard the profession. The degree should represent a competence in social work based on professional content which cannot be covered in less than two years and which includes the basic experience in class and field.

> We have made only a small beginning in bringing in public welfare in spite of increasing demands in the field. Before we go off into another specialization, we should consider what is of prime importance and exert all our efforts toward strengthening our program where the greatest need lies. Our Faculty is now greatly overworked and the bringing in of these new students will increase pressures.[20]

In defending the new training course, Florence Day pointed out that the faculty had never been able to reach agreement on what constituted basic equipment for every social worker. She said that SASS already covered in one year the material that other schools covered in two, so the second year really provided time for specialization. In the new program the home economics students would meet the School's preprofessional admission requirements and would be required to take the full first-year casework program before they began to specialize in the second year.[21]

With regard to the need for more courses in public welfare, Margaret Johnson asserted that the School would not be able to introduce more public welfare courses into the two-year program until the specializations decided what constituted basic preparation for social workers and what represented specialization within particular fields. She believed that if it were assumed that casework and group work students required a two-year course for their specialties, then there was no room in the curriculum for additional courses unless they were provided in a third year of study.[22]

Another change which attempted to unify the specializations within the School was the faculty's decision to centralize admission procedures. Under the former system of admissions each applicant was directed to a particular division of specialization when he applied to the School. While the department was considering the application, the prospective student was sent to various agencies in his chosen field to be accepted for field placement. Before he was finally admitted to the School he had to be accepted by the School *and* by a co-operating agency. The system was cumbersome, confusing, and exhausting for the student. If he were chosen by more than one agency, he had little knowledge on which to base his decision. By the time a decision was finally made, the School frequently found that it had lost a prospective student. Under the new system the student's application was received by the director of admission, who arranged an interview and gave the applicant general information about the School. The application was then forwarded to the division of specialization in which the student had indicated interest. The division of specialization could, if it desired, call the applicant in for a second interview. It was hoped that the agencies would agree to allow the School sole responsibility for the selection of students and their assignment to field placement, but this proposal ran into a roadblock of agency resistance. Not only did the agencies fear being assigned less promising students, but they also viewed the proposal as an interference with the selection of their future staff members. The ultimate decision for accepting a student remained in the hands of the division of specialization and the agency offering field placement.[23]

By 1937 it had become obvious that the School was in trouble. At a time when the demand for social workers was increasing, the student body of SASS was showing a steady decline in numbers while the enrollments at other schools of social work were on the rise. The faculty was overworked, underpaid, and disheartened. Proposals for major changes to improve the situation met opposition from within the School itself and also from co-operating agencies in the outside community. Pressure for a policy review increased when some businessmen who were active on boards of social work agencies questioned what they considered the subsidization of social work students by their agencies. In the closing months of 1937 these mounting pressures led to discussion between the School, the co-operating agencies, and the Welfare Federation about the value of social work education and the costs involved.

The principals involved in these discussions initiated a study of the School's program early in 1938.

It was decided that the primary purpose of the study should be to focus attention upon the manner in which the School is meeting the current requirements of professional education, as these are determined by changes in the field of social work practice, and to interpret the situation as found to the various individuals and groups primarily concerned. The secondary purpose was to look ahead with a view to making plans for such changes as might be indicated to enable the School to meet the changing needs of the field.[24]

This process of self-examination was to be carried out by faculty members, agency personnel, and interested laymen, who got together on working subcommittees to examine various aspects of the problem. The study was conducted under the sponsorship of a large general committee, which included prominent Clevelanders interested in social welfare problems. Each subcommittee had to find time for its already busy members to meet often enough to study and issue a report on the topic assigned to it. As the months slipped past, it became evident that there was need for professional staff assistance to help committees focus on the problems and to integrate all the material being covered in the study. The resignation of Newstetter and several other faculty members in the summer of 1938 further delayed the project.

In order to move ahead, it was decided to employ Dorothy Kahn, a leading social worker from Philadelphia, to act as resident consultant for the three-month period from October 1 to December 31, 1938. Miss Kahn used the subcommittee reports, supplemented by interviews and correspondence with leading social workers and civic leaders in Cleveland and personnel from schools of social work across the nation, to issue a broadly based evaluation of professional education for social work in Cleveland. The report was carefully organized to relate recommendations for the future to an analysis of the total educational program at the School of Applied Social Sciences. At a time when the School urgently needed to take a fresh look at its methods of education for the profession of social work, the University made a wise decision in bringing in an outside consultant who was familiar with the field and its current needs. Since Miss Kahn was without prior commitment to any single pressure group—School, agencies, or community leaders—her thorough study and diplomatic presentation went a long way toward securing agreement for the proposals she made.

One of the first ghosts that Miss Kahn laid to rest was the criticism that the co-operating agencies subsidized the students' education but failed to benefit from their investment. The study revealed that the city secured more of the school's graduates than it contributed to the total student body, and that the extremely high turnover in many of the local agencies was due to the fact that salaries for more experienced workers were not competitive with those paid in other cities. A later study of Associated Charities reported that from 1916 until the end of 1952, 904 students (public health nursing students not included) had all or a part of their training at AC; and of this group 389 were employed by the agency for more than six months. Furthermore, all those involved in the 1938 study agreed that although the student's salary during his first year might be in excess of his productivity, by the second year the student's work was more efficient and more valuable to the agency.[25]

Miss Kahn pointed out that the limited facilities of the School prevented it from coming close to meeting the increasing need for trained social workers both in the local community and in the nation. In regard to the rapidly expanding public social services, she urged that the School attempt to meet the educational needs of conscientious workers in those services who wanted to increase their understanding of social work. Recognizing the School's hesitancy to offer courses to those who had no intention of undertaking a full graduate program, she declared:

> It is the considered opinion of this observer that the profession cannot possibly suffer by sharing with those who are employed in its field whatever knowledge can be put into teachable form for this purpose, and that such activities may be constructively related to and not confused with the hard won rewards of a complete graduate curriculum.[26]

The study recognized that the chief resource of the School was

its faculty, which Miss Kahn praised as "a rare group working together with a fine esprit de corps." But she also noted that only
two other schools of social work besides SASS were represented
on the faculty, and she recommended that the School take this
imbalance into consideration when adding to the staff in the future. The study also reported that there was a real demand from
both students and agencies for a "larger complement of persons
on the faculty who hold a position of leadership in the field of social work." Miss Kahn recommended that if the School secured
faculty members with national reputations, it would not only "en-
rich the local field of social work which tends to be somewhat
ingrown," but would also be of value in attracting promising students.[27]

The question of the economical use of faculty members' time
was raised in a number of places throughout the study. Miss Kahn
thought that faculty participation in local agencies was generally
healthy, but she warned against some situations "where faculty
members seem to be in danger of being used by local social agencies as auxiliary staff, rather than colleagues or professional counsellors." The study urged that both the School and the agencies
guard against practices which take faculty members away from
their main function of furthering professional education. Another
large drain on faculty members' time was the long hours spent
advising students on their general education and on their theses.
Pointing out that a professional graduate school was a place where
"independence and maturity should be expected and encouraged," Miss Kahn suggested that the existing advisory system
should be more carefully examined.[28]

The need for economy of manpower was directly related to the
study's recommendations regarding further centralization of the
School's administrative processes. Because of the confusion regarding policy-making and administrative functions, which were
largely handled by committees, the decision-making process was
unnecessarily prolonged. Miss Kahn recommended an organizational revision of the School's administration along functional lines
and a sharper delineation between administrative responsibilities
and policy-making decisions.[29]

The administrative weaknesses which Miss Kahn noted were due to a number of factors—lack of unity in the educational program, the vested interests of those in separate departments, the heavy reliance upon a labyrinth of committees and subcommittees for administration, and the dean's tendency to mull over decisions in his slow and deliberate fashion. Yet these problems could have been solved by a combination of thought and forcefulness on the part of the faculty and the university. What could not be changed by the educational personnel of the School alone was the dominant method of field training, the remunerative plan, which impeded both the centralization of administration and the development of a generic curriculum.

Although Miss Kahn wrote that "when the School was first organized a carefully thought-out plan of cooperation was put into effect," this was hardly so. The School simply took over the training program at Associated Charities as its first course in social work. Students in the course were considered staff members, who were paid a salary and were required to remain with the agency for one year after they completed their one-year course of training. When the casework program became a two-year course, students were encouraged by the agency to write their theses in the third year because the demands of a full-time job and course work left no time for research and writing. The School of Applied Social Sciences became widely known for this plan of field placement, which became known as the "Cooperative Plan" or the "Remunerative Plan." In the early years the School pointed with pride to the plan, which not only financed the students' professional education but also encouraged a mature sense of responsibility toward the agency. But Miss Sydnor Walker's criticism that the plan was nothing but the old apprenticeship method in academic disguise was an echo that was heard with increasing stridency during the late 1920's and the 1930's. As the system came under attack, those who favored the plan began to develop an intellectual rationale for the School's approach. First, they pointed to the "cooperative plan" which had been developed at the University of Cincinnati to enable engineering students to spend alternate weeks at the school and in the manufacturing plants of the city. Later they pointed out that it was common practice for medical students to gain practical experience in hospitals.[30]

But there was increasing unrest among the faculty about the School's overemphasis on practical training at the expense of academic education. Most students were not able to finish their theses in the second year, and a large number never did receive their degrees. In 1930 the faculty voted to press for the adoption of a plan providing three days a week field placement and two days a week in the classroom, but 1930 was not a propitious year for such a major change. There was also some attempt to provide more than one field-placement experience for family case-work students; but despite the fact that a broader experience in the field had proved successful for students in medical social work and group work, the School was not able to establish such a program for students in other divisions. In her report Miss Kahn pointed out that the agencies involved in the remunerative plan believed:

> With twenty-one months of continuous work in a single agency, students are better prepared for agency work and know the agency so well when they begin on their period of employment that they do not require a period of orientation.[31]

Nevertheless, the Depression had brought developments which eventually forced a re-examination of the remunerative plan. The creation of the Cuyahoga County Relief Administration in 1933 suddenly changed the function of the private agencies which had been responsible for dispensing relief funds. The impact of the change was immediately felt in the School. While the Associated Charities had been the chief agency for distributing relief in the county, the AC had had over 90 students placed in its offices; but by the summer of 1933 the entire professional staff of Associated Charities numbered only 53, which included just 12 second-year students in placement. Attempts to place students in public agencies were not always successful, although in the fall of 1934 the Federal Emergency Relief Administration financed a special program for the placement of 41 students in public agencies. Part of the trouble with public placements was related to civil service regulations, and the School's reluctance to adjust to these regulations by developing a block plan for field placements; but a good deal of the difficulty was caused by the attitude of Governor Martin L. Davey. It was Dean Cutler who referred to "the governor of a certain mid-western state . . . [who views] . . . social workers in the public service as persistent job-holders who refuse to be classified as either Democrats or Republicans."[32] There was an urgent need to provide more field placements for students—not only with public agencies, but also with a greater number of private ones.

Miss Kahn noted that the problems and discussions related to the remunerative plan were largely responsible for organization of the study. Her report dealt not only with the educational questions raised by the plan, but also with the total problem of costs— costs to the agency related to training students, and the cost to the student of financing his education. After pointing out the technical difficulty of determining the cost to the agencies of training students, Miss Kahn arrived at a figure of $346.11, which indicated the average net cost for field work training per student for one year. Essentially this figure represented the difference between the amount of work done by a student and that done by a full-time worker, after taking into consideration the salary which was paid to the student. Miss Kahn pointed out that the total amount calculated on this basis was less than two-tenths of one per cent of the total expenditures of the agencies in the community, and she concluded:

> Thus whatever may be said of these costs agency by agency, the total investment made by the community in professional education is an infinitesimal part of the total expenditures for social services. If to this were added the net cost to the University, i.e. $317.60 per student per year, the cost is still less than one half of one percent of total costs.
>
> The community can well afford, therefore, to concentrate its attention on methods of securing the best results in preparing workers for the assumption of grave responsibilities, rather than on the size of the expenditure.[33]

Having demonstrated the community's responsibility for financing field placements, Miss Kahn added that it was the consensus of everyone who participated in the study that any immediate change in the plan should not be accompanied by a change in the

Outreach Worker, Associated Charities Style

The Friendly Visitor

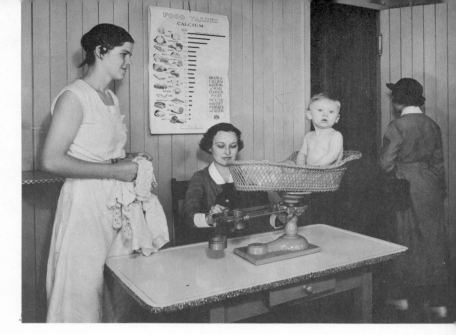

Child Welfare

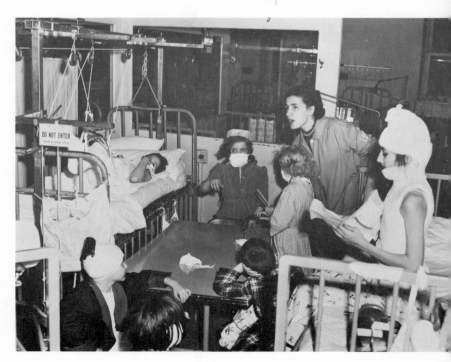

Group Work in a Hospital Setting

SASS, the School of Little Houses

Dean James E. Cutler

Dean Leonard W. Mayo

Dean Margaret Johnson

Coffee Break in Beaumont Hall Lounge

Margaret Allen Ireland Library

Classroom, Beaumont Hall

Dean Nathan E. Cohen

Dean Herman D. Stein

Beaumont Hall

outlay of the agencies for this purpose. Financial aid was important for students, and the School was widely known for its plan of student aid. If the amount of money available for student aid were suddenly withdrawn, a consequent reduction in the number of students would not only hurt the School, but would also endanger future recruitment for local agencies.[34]

Miss Kahn listed the advantages and disadvantages of the remunerative plan. The advantages centered around the agencies' preference for training students whom they had selected for their own staff and familiarized with their own agency. The disadvantages listed by Miss Kahn were primarily educational. Her criticisms included these observations:

1] The plan requires that the whole program of education be adapted to the requirements of particular agencies, rather than to the whole field of social work, which it is the School's function to serve.
2] It limits the educational experience to a single field placement, and makes mobility between fields difficult.
3] The student carries too heavy a load in attempting to be a student and a staff member at the same time; moreover, he is compelled to choose his field work and agency at a point when he is not prepared to do so.
4] The attempts to match students to remunerative places in the agency makes the selection of students difficult and sometimes results in losing good material because it cannot be fitted into a particular agency's available staff opening.

    . . . .

If there is no other change as a result of this study, it is clear that there is an imperative necessity for change in this plan, however gradual it may be.[35]

Miss Kahn advocated as an alternative to the remunerative plan that any funds available for student aid be clearly identified as scholarship funds, to be awarded on the basis of merit and need. While the eventual aim should be to secure an adequate endowment for this purpose at the School of Applied Social Sciences, Miss Kahn suggested that during the interim the agencies use the funds for remuneration already available for scholarships to be administered by the Welfare Federation. Her final recommendations listed three changes:

1) Encourage immediate separation of field work from stipends to students.
2) Arrange for more than one field work experience for most if not all students.
3) Abandon the remunerative plan in favor of scholarships.[36]

Although the section of the report which dealt with the curriculum indicated more general satisfaction with this aspect of the School's educational program, the report did suggest important curricular revisions to keep the School abreast of changes in the field of social work. Observing that "the concentration to date in faculty selection as well as in curriculum [had] been on preparation for private social agencies," Miss Kahn reported that all the participants in the study agreed that students needed to be given more material in public welfare. There was also a need within the field of social work for course material covering current social problems, the relationship of social workers to social action, social welfare administration, methods of interpretation and publicity, and social work in rural areas.[37]

The report stressed the need for a greater correlation of course material; there was a particularly strong need to relate courses in social case work to courses in public welfare, and vice versa. Miss Kahn went on to point the way toward a more generic approach that would include:

1] Further effort in the direction of a general basic curriculum with less separation between the parts of the case work field.
2] More emphasis on basic training for social work with less on specialization.
3] Closer correlation between courses dealing with the individual, with social work practice, and with industrial problems and cultural backgrounds.[38]

In relation to local needs within the field of social work, the report urged that the School establish more field placements in both public and private agencies. Miss Kahn also recommended that the curriculum be made more flexible by providing more advanced courses for those with degrees in social work and more basic courses for those already practicing without social work education.[39]

Miss Kahn raised other important problems facing the School.

The completely inadequate basement library was not just musty—
it was frequently flooded; and the five little houses that comprised
the physical plant of the School were so run-down that they provided a field experience in poverty conditions which the School
had yet to catalogue. While Miss Kahn noted that it was "significant of the professional spirit of the School that it was found difficult to secure discussion of the problems of physical equipment,"
she suggested that the School's impending twenty-fifth anniversary might provide the occasion for securing funds for a modern
structure which would more economically care for the physical
needs of the School. She also recommended that students be
charged a five-dollar library fee to help build up the library. In
considering the relationship between the School and the entire
university, Miss Kahn recommended that an effort be made to
"break down the comparative isolation of the School from University life," and she suggested that the School form a general advisory committee to help in interpreting the program and needs of
the School to the university administration.[40]

In general the Kahn Study was well received by the School, the
social work field, and the laymen interested in social welfare.
Those faculty members who had been pressing for a more generic
approach less dictated by the short-term requirements of the agencies strove to implement its suggestions. Despite some misgivings
about the ending of the remunerative plan, the agencies co-operated with the School in providing scholarships and field placements for students. Equally important was their co-operation in a
policy which vested the placement of students and the disburse-
ment of scholarship funds in the hands of the School. Laymen
demonstrated their support of the study by recommending its
conclusions to the boards of agencies on which they served and
by helping to increase the community's financial support of the
School. All of these changes were not accomplished overnight.
Many of the proposals were resisted by both faculty members and
agency executives, and it took the passage of time and several
faculty changes before all of the major recommendations of the
study were incorporated into the School's program.

Before there was even time to start working on the proposed

changes, the School of Applied Social Sciences almost went out of existence for a second time. By the beginning of the year 1940, the School's accumulated indebtedness had risen to nearly $60,000, and the estimated deficit for that year was another $30,000. To make matters worse, the faculty was bogged down in seemingly endless discussion about the reorganization of the School, while Dean Cutler feared that there were "grave dangers that might result from any widespread effort at internal reorganization." The university administration and its board of trustees were also troubled by the difficulties within the School and by "the apparent inability of the School to operate within its assured income." On June 11, 1940, the university trustees voted that "the School of Applied Social Sciences be continued throughout 1940-1941 with the understanding that if by the spring of 1941 the financial problems of the School do not seem any nearer solution the School shall be discontinued at that time." A meeting of the SASS faculty demonstrated the impact of this decision: it put them "face to face with reality." The dean, who had been troubled with illness, was clearly not up to the task which the School had to undertake if it were to survive. Following consultations with members of the faculty, the Welfare Federation, and the president of the university, Dean Cutler decided to retire at the end of the 1940-41 school year.

During the summer and fall of 1940 the School made an intensive search for a person to fill the vacancy. The mandate given to the search committee was to look for candidates who would have not only the qualifications for heading the School, but could also conduct a successful drive to build a firm financial base for it. The final choice was Leonard W. Mayo. He had an excellent background in social work administration and had also been a faculty member at the New York School of Social Work. Under his leadership the School of Applied Social Sciences began to climb out of the financial and administrative bog in which it had been immersed for the preceding few years.

NOTES

[1] Roy Lubove, *The Professional Altruist: The Emergence of Social Work as a Career, 1880-1930* (Cambridge: Harvard University Press, 1965), chap. V, *passim*.

[2] James E. Cutler, "Notes on Speech before SASS Students" (undated, but apparently given in the first years of the School).

[3] Waite, 91.

[4] Quoted in Lubove, 113.

[5] Waite, 220.

[6] Nathan E. Cohen, *Social Work in the American Tradition* (New York: Holt, Rinehart and Winston, 1958), 158.

[7] Quoted in Sara Elizabeth Maloney, "The Development of Group Work Education in the Schools of Social Work in the United States" (unpublished Ph.D. dissertation, The School of Applied Social Sciences, Western Reserve University, 1963), 170.

[8] *Ibid.* Professor Maloney's work clearly shows the great influence of those who had their training at SASS during these years. They were missionaries of group work in many parts of the nation, and it is clear that SASS was indeed a pioneering institution in the establishment of group work as an integral part of the social work profession.

[9] James E. Cutler and Maurice R. Davie, *A Study in Professional Education at Western Reserve University: The School of Applied Social Sciences, 1916-1930* (Cleveland: The Press of Western Reserve University, 1930), 55.

[10] Waite, 221, 224.

[11] *Ibid.*, 232-83; Dorothy C. Kahn, "A Study of Professional Education for Social Work in Cleveland" (mimeographed, 1938), 77.

[12] General Faculty, "Minutes," November 24, 1933; Faculty as Committee of the Whole, "Minutes," November 3, 1934.

[13] General Faculty, "Minutes," December 7, 1934.

[14] "Notes on Criticism of Training Program at School of Applied Social Sciences, W.R.U." (submitted by an individual alumnus to the Alumni Round Table), February 18, 1936.

[15] *Ibid.*

[16] *Ibid.*

[17] *Ibid.*

[18] Case Work Alumni, "Minutes," February 18, 1936; March 31, 1936.

[19] General Faculty, "Minutes," May, 1937 to June 8, 1938.

[20] General Faculty, "Minutes," April 22, 1938.

[21] *Ibid.*

[22] *Ibid.*

[23] Joint meeting of Consulting Staff in Child Welfare and Supervisors of Stu-

dents in Child Welfare, "Minutes," March 3, 1937; Consulting Staff in Child Welfare, "Minutes," February, 1937.

24 Kahn, 1.

25 *Ibid.*, 8-11; Waite, 326; Helen W. Hanchette, "Proposed Change in Training Program As It Affects Our Agency" (mimeographed, April 10, 1939).

26 Kahn, 11-14.

27 *Ibid.*, 32-33.

28 *Ibid.*, 33-34, 40-41.

29 *Ibid.*, 42-45.

30 James E. Cutler, "Our Own School," a paper read at a faculty seminar on professional education, October 26, 1928; Cutler and Davie, 26-30.

31 Kahn, 55.

32 James E. Cutler, "Social Work and Societal Evolution," *Studies in the Science of Society*, ed. George P. Murdock (New Haven: Yale University Press, 1937), 118-19.

33 Kahn, 53-54.

34 *Ibid.*, 54.

35 *Ibid.*, 55-57.

36 *Ibid.*, 57-59.

37 *Ibid.*, 35-39.

38 *Ibid.*, 38.

39 *Ibid.*, 39-40.

40 *Ibid.*, 60-62, 70-71.

V.   Consolidation

One of the major contributions of Leonard Mayo was his ability to raise financial support for the School. While there was no major increase in endowment during his deanship from 1941 to 1948, Mayo was successful in securing funds to cover a major portion of the School's annual deficit as well as substantial commitments of money for the construction of a new building. Even before he became dean, he contacted many nationally known foundations in New York as a part of the School's campaign to raise $60,000 for operations during the next two years. As soon as he arrived in Cleveland he began to contact wealthy citizens and corporations to explain the School's role in social welfare. He found that many members of the community regarded "social workers as those who [were] engaged to protect the relief recipients from the attacks of the taxpayer," and "his emphasis on the broader aspects of social work, particularly its preventative and rehabilitative aspects, came as a complete surprise to many people."[1] Mayo's approach was expressed in language that the businessman would understand; his interpretation of the role of social workers was buttressed by facts and figures demonstrating the economy of using trained personnel in the welfare field. His letters to community leaders were frequently followed by interviews in which he stressed that technical training was as important in social work as it was in business and industry. With his aggressive enthusiasm he was successful in persuading many Clevelanders to discharge their civic responsibility by contributing to the education of social workers who dealt with community problems.

Not only did Mayo secure the support of influential laymen, but he also won the respect of the city's social agencies. By 1942 there were fifty agencies providing field placements for the School—double the number of four years earlier. Mayo's skill in public relations and community organization drew him into positions of leadership on both the local and national scenes. His national activities and speaking engagements served to publicize SASS, which in turn helped the School recruit students and faculty members from all over the country.

Mayo's effective interpretation of social work education also promoted a closer relationship between SASS and the university community. He quickly established good rapport with the president and trustees of the university as well as with faculty members from other schools and departments. This rapport strengthened the School's working relationship with other disciplines that contributed to the educational program for social workers. In a memorandum to President Leutner, Mayo pointed with pride to the increased co-operation with the medical school that had been achieved during his last year as dean:

> One of the most significant developments having to do with relations within the University, is the agreement recently entered into by which the School of Applied Social Sciences will nominate and provide appointments on its faculty for the Director of Social Service and the supervisors of Medical and Psychiatric Social Work in University Hospitals; and the further reciprocal arrangement by which the School of Medicine will nominate and provide appointments for those who are to teach courses at the School of Applied Social Sciences in Medical Information and Psychiatry. In addition, the Psychiatric Clinic of University Hospitals and the Department of Medicine of the School of Medicine have appointed a member of the Clinic staff to act as a liaison with the faculty of the School of Applied Social Sciences. He will have an appointment on the faculty of the School and be available on specific days each month to work with the Curriculum Committee and the subcommittee on psychiatric content. Through this liaison, the School of Medicine will make its nominations of the people who will teach our course in Psychiatry and Medical Information.[2]

This arrangement, which was worked out by Leonard Mayo in 1947, was to prove of invaluable assistance seven years later, when the School integrated its courses to establish a generic "core" curriculum. On the other hand, this relationship with the medical school reinforced the analytical approach to social work at a time when the field was beginning to incorporate new knowledge from the social sciences.

However, a short-lived attempt to establish a vocational-guidance training program in co-operation with the psychology department demonstrated that interdisciplinary projects were not

always very successful. The chairman of the psychology department wrote to Mayo that he believed the methods, techniques,
and philosophy of vocational guidance were primarily psychological. He continued:

> We believe that training in social work does not fit the person to
> do vocational guidance. I have been long struck with the fact that
> the ideology of the social worker and that of the psychologist are
> in many respects antithetical, although this is not intended as a
> criticism of either discipline. Our interest is in the scientific study
> and analysis of the individual. We believe that this is the only
> sound basis for a program which presumes to help people. If you
> place the emphasis first upon helping people, or doing good, the sci-
> entific approach is often forgotten or pushed into the background.[3]

Mayo noted on the psychologist's memorandum that these were
"fighting words." Although there were further discussions between
the departments, the co-operative vocational-guidance program
petered out after a few years.

Within the School, Mayo moved on the recommendations of the
Kahn report to integrate the organizational structure of SASS. Although many of the administrative functions of the departments
of specialization had been formally abandoned before Mayo arrived, the tendency to think in terms of specializations lingered
on. Until 1940 policy decisions had been made by a committee
composed of the directors of the specializations and the dean.
Through Mayo's initiative the general faculty took over responsibility for determining policy. Standing committees were appointed to review and develop programs and practices in areas
such as curriculum, admissions, and thesis requirements; but these
committees had to report back to the general faculty for approval
of policy changes. A new administrative committee was established to organize the teaching staff, to act as a co-ordinating body
for the other committees, and to make interim decisions on situations that required immediate attention. The new organizational
structure was designed not only to broaden the base of faculty
power, but also to provide further integration of the social work
faculty. Mayo was careful to appoint faculty members from each
of the former specializations to serve on the new committees.
Manuals on the thesis requirement and field work procedure were

revised by joint committees which included representatives from the field work agencies. The former advisory committees (of laymen) and consulting committees (of agency representatives) that had been organized around the specializations were abandoned in favor of a single advisory committee responsible directly to the School. It was composed of twelve "informed citizens, interested both in education and social work and in the broad problems of social welfare of this community." The advisory committee's function was "to work closely with the School of Applied Social Sciences on problems of program and financing."

This horizontal reorganization went a long way toward integrating social work education within the School. Even more might have been accomplished in relation to the integration of the curriculum and of field work practice had not the entrance of the United States into World War II diverted the attention of both the dean and the faculty.

Shortly after Pearl Harbor Mayo was called upon to become assistant director of the Cuyahoga County Civilian Defense Department and two years later the University was asked to release him on a part-time basis so he might become director of Civilian Mobilization in Cuyahoga County. For six months he could spend only two days a week at the School. In 1945 Mayo became chairman of the Metropolitan Development Council, and throughout his tenure as dean he served on numerous committees that were set up to handle the national emergency and the postwar adjustment. Many of the faculty of SASS were similarly involved in wartime activities, with the result that the School faced a considerable turnover of its faculty and had to employ a number of part-time teachers during the 1940's.

The war brought a martial atmosphere to the university, whose facilities were used for an Army Air Corps training center. SASS lost some of its best offices to air force personnel, and the favorite joke among social work students was the call for a "better relationship" between the shouting drill sergeant and his "group." A great decrease in the number of male students at SASS was accompanied by a tremendous increase in the School's special programs to meet the wartime needs of the community and the nation. In the summer of 1942 SASS adopted a trimester system to enable students to finish the established twenty-one month program in sixteen months. During the same period a modified "block plan" of field placement was organized to allow some students to get their practical experience in agencies outside of the Cleveland area. After the war the School wanted to extend this system of field placement under an academic calendar that was divided into quarters, but the university decided that all of its schools would return to the semester calendar. By the fall of 1946 SASS had terminated its accelerated program.

Many of the educational developments at SASS were designed to meet the problems that faced the community as a result of the war. Relief problems that had plagued the nation for more than a decade began to fade away like a bad dream, but the social upheavals of wartime intensified the need for trained social workers. The nation was shocked to learn that 7.6 per cent of its draftees were rejected for mental or emotional reasons. Family separations and an increase in juvenile delinquency brought a new kind of client to social agencies. The recruitment of women into the nation's factories brought increased concern about "latchkey" children, and after the war the return of service men and women from the armed forces was accompanied by problems of adjustment to civilian society. The School of Applied Social Sciences responded with great resourcefulness to provide special courses and institutes for staff workers and volunteers faced with these new social problems.

The wartime expansion of USO centers and traditional group-work settings brought an increased demand for staff with recreational skills, and the School also attempted to meet these community needs. In 1944 SASS opened a new studio in the basement of Euclid Hall to provide arts and crafts equipment for group work students. Actually the School's inclusion of courses on program skills was already a subject of criticism by those who wished to concentrate on the professional aspects of social work education. As one faculty member later recalled, the revolt began in the 1930's when a conscientious lecturer posted a notice on the School's bulletin board informing all group work students that they were to learn the correct words of the song, "Chickadee, My Chickadee." Nevertheless, many of the group work agencies believed that program skills were essential, and it was not until 1955 that these courses were removed from the School's catalogue.

In addition to the School's major efforts to meet wartime needs, attention was also given to expediting the Kahn report's recommendations regarding the field of public welfare. In 1944 Mayo was able to report:

> During the last two years we have added two courses in Public Welfare and are making every effort to add appropriate Public Welfare material to the content of other courses. The fact that we have no courses at present in the social insurances is a serious lack which we plan to meet in the fall. During the current semester we are offering a special section of our "Introduction to Social Case Work" for staff members of the Cleveland Regional Office of the State Division on Aid to the Aged. Last summer we offered a week's institute for staff members of the Public Welfare Department of this and other states. We are offering a similar but longer institute this summer in which the Division of Social Welfare of the State of Ohio has expressed great interest. We have also offered several week-end institutes this last winter and spring for staff members of local, county and state Departments of Public Welfare.
>
>   . . . .
>
> It is encouraging to report that the Cuyahoga County Relief Department has recently modified a plan of long standing under which each student in training was required to assume responsibility for fifty families on relief. The new plan stipulates that beginning students may confine their efforts to only fifteen families, thus providing a far more effective learning experience.[4]

The end of the war saw a sharp increase in the enrollment at SASS. The School was delighted with the large percentage of male students who entered under the G.I. educational bill. But by 1949 the enrollment of veterans had fallen off, and the McCarthyism of the early fifties also served to discourage student involvement in social welfare.

In 1948 Dean Mayo left SASS to become vice-president of Western Reserve University. His successor, Donald V. Wilson, remained in office for just one year, and Margaret Johnson was appointed the new dean in 1950. Miss Johnson had been one of the first graduates of the School of Applied Social Sciences. After working in personnel management in industry and holding executive positions in the local and national League of Women Voters, Miss Johnson became executive secretary of the School in 1927. In 1930 she was appointed assistant dean, and throughout the years before 1950 she served as acting dean on a number of occasions.

It was especially fitting that the School finally moved into a building of its own during the period of Miss Johnson's leadership. She had been a student when the School's first classes were held in two dingy rooms on the Adelbert College campus, and had played an important part in the development of the School in succeeding years. The Alumni Association, which she had helped to form in the early 1930's and had served as secretary until she became dean, contributed both time and money to secure a decent building to house their school. Finally, in 1951, the School of Applied Social Sciences moved into a new building on Abington Road. It was named Beaumont Hall in honor of the Beaumont Foundation, which had contributed a major part of the money which financed its building.

The decade of the 1950's was a significant period for Western Reserve University. In 1949 John S. Millis came to Cleveland to become the president of a university whose political structure resembled a medieval kingdom. Instead of dukes and barons, there were deans and full professors who held on to their authority with all the tenacity of feudal lords. Millis, who did not regard himself as first among equals, had some of the characteristics of the granite of Vermont—the state from whence he came. His efforts to unify the university and develop graduate and professional schools that would be the best in the midwest brought an end to the semiautonomy that had existed within the university's departments, colleges, and professional schools.

The new president took a critical look at SASS during his first year in office. As usual, the financial situation was not good. A deficit of over $60,000 (38 per cent of the total budget) had to be met out of the university's General Funds in 1950. In examining these costs President Millis questioned the ratio of faculty to students at the School. Taking into account the fact that students attended the School only two days out of five, he calculated that

the ratio was about one faculty member to four students, whereas
he believed that it was possible to use the tutorial method with a
staff ratio of ten to one. Millis also examined the School's policy of
promotions in light of his own conviction that promotions "must
be justified upon the grounds of unusual contributions as a teacher
and/or scholar."

The president advised Dean Johnson that SASS must tighten
its budget, and then he himself moved to strengthen the community's support of the School by reorganizing the Advisory Committee on a broader base. When 1951 brought a further decrease
in the number of students, which was accompanied by an even
larger deficit, President Millis examined more closely the time-
consuming activities of the faculty. He saw a major weakness in
the organizational structure of the School—a proliferation of committees which demanded a great deal of faculty time. He also
questioned the amount of time spent in advising students and was
critical of the faculty's tendency to consider its service to community organizations as part of the educational process. Lastly,
he believed that a professional school should be more involved in
productive research.

In the spring of 1952 President Millis directed Dean Johnson to
"organize her faculty to conduct a searching study of the program
and operations of the School." While he emphasized that the basic
purpose of the study was "to improve the quality of social work
education," he requested that the faculty clearly define the objectives of the School, evaluate its current program in light of these
objectives, and make whatever changes were necessary. Although
the faculty was not sure that the president fully understood the
profession and its educational process, his request for a searching
study was welcomed by the many faculty members who were
eager to engage in a thorough examination of education for social
work. Major social changes, such as the increasing role of government in the welfare services, were producing "widespread and
urgent demand for social workers prepared to use their skills in
new settings and in new problem areas." Just a year earlier the
National Council on Social Work Education had issued a major
report on education "in relation to the responsibility of social work

in the broad field of social welfare" (*Social Work Education in the United States* by Ernest V. Hollis and Alice L. Taylor).

SASS had, in fact, kept abreast of broad national developments in the field of social work education. By 1946 the curriculum included the "basic eight" areas of study established by the American Association of Schools of Social Work in 1944. These eight fields consisted of casework, group work, community organization, public welfare, social administration, social research, medical information, and psychiatric information. But self-scrutiny was an ongoing process among those on the frontiers of a young profession:

> Events within the School itself during the last two years had sharpened the critical sensibilities of the faculty to shortcomings in the program and had gradually induced a readiness for change. The inauguration of the Advanced Program in the autumn of 1951 had entailed countless hours of study and discussion. The numerous consultations with leaders in social work practice, social work education and the social sciences during the first year of the Advanced Program stimulated both the imagination and the energy of the faculty. The discussions with Doctor Young and Doctor Cottrell of the Russell Sage Foundation, had brought home to the faculty the question of whether the School was proceeding on too narrow a conceptual base in its current program, and had convinced many members of the faculty of the need for a more extensive and thoroughgoing integration of the newer contributions of the social sciences in the basic curriculum of the School.[5]

The 1952 study of the School of Applied Social Sciences was conducted entirely by the faculty without the assistance of a paid consultant or administrator. There is no question that this was the most soul-searching examination of its program that the School had ever undertaken. National leaders in social work education, practitioners in the field, alumni, and students were all consulted about the educational program of the School. The research was followed by months of hard work on carefully organized and coordinated committees which studied and prepared proposals on all aspects of the School's operation. All of this was done by faculty members in addition to their regular schedule of responsibilities. The complex process of the study not only reflected the faculty's commitment to the School, but also demonstrated the ability to use its knowledge of the group process. The rewards were commensurate with the effort. The Hollis and Taylor study points out:

> Educationally sound curriculum proposals can, of course, be developed without regard for the professional readiness of the human beings concerned. Indeed, history shows this to have been a cardinal error in the strategy of those who heretofore have developed social work curricula. . . . Valid curricula may be developed for "the best of all possible worlds," but they should be introduced with a due regard for faculty and student limitations. Participation in program development is a sure way to increase professional readiness.[6]

When President Millis' directive arrived in the spring of 1952, a statistical analysis of the School's student body during a recent academic year was already under way. The report of this research was given serious attention by the faculty as it prepared to begin the study. The analysis was concerned with demographic characteristics, social class distribution, and evidence of ability. The researcher believed that the study revealed several implications for the School. Noting that three-fourths of the students were middle class and assuming a significant difference between middle class and lower class culture, he suggested that the curriculum should contain more material on cultural anthropology. The analysis further indicated that 10 per cent of the students had I.Q. ratings below 110 on high school tests and over 40 per cent of the students ranked below the 75th percentile in their high school classes. The researcher seriously questioned whether those with I.Q.'s under 110 should be in graduate school at all, and he believed that unless college records showed marked improvement, it was doubtful if the second group would do high-grade graduate work. The last section of the analysis compared ranking by SASS advisers with the I.Q. and college rank scores, and demonstrated great discrepancy between faculty evaluation of students and test and rank criteria. The implications for the School's admission policies and advisory program were obvious.[7]

In the early days of the self-study the faculty's executive committee decided that it would be useful to learn what former students thought about their educational experience at SASS. A questionnaire was sent to a random sample of 20 per cent of the students from each graduating class between 1940 and 1952. The response, which came from 47 per cent of those contacted, revealed "the very limited intellectual outlook of far too many" of the students and raised serious questions about the graduates' "comprehension of the fields of related knowledge which provide the intellectual and technical framework of social work education." One question asked the graduates to discuss the implication for social work education of the broad social changes which had occurred in the world during the last few decades. Although there were a few answers which the faculty considered good, some students simply did not understand the question and others "could not see the world forest for the social work trees." Another question asked the graduates whether their preparation had been adequate with respect to the "scientific knowledge of the nature and process of human behavior." The responses indicated that the respondents' concepts of scientific knowledge related to human behavior were limited almost exclusively to psychiatry.[8]

While those answering the questionnaire were most enthusiastic about the educational value of their field-work experience, less than half believed that the technical courses (casework, group work, and community organization) in their fields of specialization were good. Furthermore, many of the respondents were critical of the failure of the School's program to integrate classroom and field work experience. These criticisms were especially disturbing because the School had always believed that one of its strong points was the high level of its technical training; and the system of faculty advising, which was praised by the respondents, was supposed to be an important tool in integrating the theory and practice of social work.[9]

The first major effort of the self-study was to define the objectives of the School of Applied Sciences. While it was agreed that the most important purpose of the School was, and always had been, to produce competent social workers through "a program of education which provides students with a specialized body of knowledge and skill and with the professional ethics and philosophy essential to the practice of their profession," there were three additional objectives which the study committee believed had been less consciously pursued in the past—contribution to professional knowledge through research, participation in appropriate professional and scientific bodies, and involvement within the university setting. The latter objectives were defined not only to clarify the role of the faculty, but also to direct attention to the need for providing time for these responsibilities.[10]

In order to achieve the objective of training competent social workers, the faculty recognized that it was necessary to take into account broad changes in the contemporary world. It is evident that the study committee gave careful attention to the review of the field of social welfare that was contained in the Hollis and Taylor study. The study considered the role of social workers in relationship to factors such as (1) major social changes in the world and the role of the United States in international co-operation and leadership, (2) multiplying problems of urbanized society, (3) changes in the social agencies in which social work is performed, (4) changes in the practice of social work, and (5) changes and developments in the sciences and professions upon which social work draws for its knowledge. Recognizing contemporary developments such as these, the faculty was anxious to give students a broader base of scientific knowledge and a deeper understanding of the world around them. Rather than engaging in a singular re-examination of the patchwork quilt of courses that had been developed to meet the needs of the field over the years, the study committee decided to revise the curriculum by identifying broad areas of knowledge that were important for the education of social workers in the contemporary world.[11]

As the faculty members met in committees and struggled with the task before them, certain basic assumptions about social work education emerged to give direction to the establishment of a core curriculum. Grace Coyle, whose broad comprehension of professional education made her a leader in the study process, outlined these assumptions in a paper delivered to the National Council on Social Work Education. While practice courses remained central in the curriculum, they needed to be "balanced and supported by other equally important courses." Essential to social work education were "an identification with the tradition and purposes of the profession, a concern for the provision of adequate social services and the improvement of the social milieu." The second assumption identified the relationship between social work and certain underlying bodies of knowledge. While social work was dependent on the fields of biology, psychology, medicine, and psychiatry to understand the individual, it was equally important to incorporate knowledge from social sciences such as anthropology, sociology, social psychology, economics, and political science to provide the social worker with an understanding of society and culture. A third assumption was that all students should be impressed with the importance of research, not just as an academic discipline, but as a way of thinking about social work practice. The fourth assumption was that field practice needed to be correlated with the entire curriculum, not just the practice courses. In conclusion, Miss Coyle wrote:

> Finally, our struggles to remake the curriculum brought us again and again to a conviction that we needed more continued and consistent effort to develop and transmit the body of values and philosophy which should guide the social worker. . . . If the social services are to gain and hold an adequate place in the modern world, if they are to function in the interests of peace and progress internationally, if practice is to be guided wisely not only in its relations to individuals but in its public policies, students must find in their education well defined and defensible philosophy.
>
> . . . .
>
> These four assumptions are not formulations made or accepted by our faculty. They are rather a distillation of the hours of committee discussions we have been through. . . . We are certainly not presenting them as new educational discoveries but perhaps as indicators of the foundations upon which the new curriculum was built.[12]

The core curriculum which was finally developed attempted to give students "a basic core of knowledge concerning society, social work methods and the purposes of social work in society." The philosophy of social work was to permeate the student's entire educational experience, but it was given added emphasis in a fourth-semester seminar in social work during which the student was helped to integrate the total content of his class and field learning with his role as a professional person in the field of social work.[13]

Knowledge of the individual and the dynamics of human behavior were included in a four-semester sequence which included course material in medicine, psychiatry, and psychology. The sequence was developed in close co-operation with the medical school and was to some extent influenced by the new program for educating medical students which had recently been developed by that school. During the first year emphasis was placed on the normal growth and development of the individual from conception to death, and during the second year psychopathology and physical illness were traced in the same order. The sequence was taught by a team of experts composed of specialists in medicine (including psychiatry), psychologists, and a member of the SASS faculty. In tracing the physical, emotional, social, and intellectual development of a human being, care was taken to include case material from social work practice whenever possible.[14]

A parallel sequence of material from related sciences was offered during the first two semesters under the name Dynamics of Social Process. Material for the course, which was designed to give students an understanding of structure and social process in the community and in groups, was drawn from basic concepts of sociology, cultural anthropology, and social psychology. After consultation with social workers in the field and other schools of social work, the course was developed by the faculty, with the help of a sociologist attached to the School, as a part of the Russell Sage Research Project.[15]

The four-semester sequence of courses in Social Welfare Organization drew on content previously contained in such courses as Public Welfare, History of Social Work, Introduction to Community Organization, and Law. The four major divisions included in the sequence were (1) the historical roots and development of social work as a response to social conditions, (2) the contemporary scene in social welfare organization, (3) the use of the social agency to implement a social purpose, and (4) the profession and the professional person (the fourth semester of this sequence was the seminar in social work).[16]

A six-hour sequence in research, given during the second year, was designed not only to teach research methodology but also to develop conviction about the place of research in social work. The fourth semester of this sequence was a two-credit-hour group project seminar, which the faculty hoped would "enable the student to develop a more critical approach to daily practice and an ability to be an intelligent consumer of research."[17] Electives were offered in advanced psychodynamics, social work in multidisciplinary agencies, and administration.

The development of all the sequences in the new curriculum followed a five-month period of consultation with field instructors and selected practitioners who contributed to determining the goals of the master's program in light of what current practice would require of the graduate. These consultations were especially helpful in working out the areas to be covered in the practice courses—both in the classroom and in the field. Reorganization of the practice courses provided that caseworkers and group workers take a four-semester classroom sequence in their areas of specialization, as well as taking single courses in the two major practice areas outside their specializations.[18] The first five weeks of the first-semester practice course were devoted to a general introduction to social work practice which stressed the common core of knowledge and skill essential for all social workers. Thus, during the beginning of the student's education and again in the fourth-semester seminar in social work, specific attention was given to the generic concepts of social work. During the first year emphasis was placed on "everyday situations faced by families and individuals, which would include major activities and experiences in life as influenced by social, cultural, and economic factors." During the first year the faculty in both casework and group work courses concentrated on helping the student acquire a scientific or problem-solving approach. In the second year the student was given more complicated problems in diagnostic formulation and treatment.[19]

The study committee engaged in a thorough review of the School's program for field work. Operating on the assumption that the School must provide as much correlation between field practice and course content as possible, the faculty chose to continue using the concurrent plan of field practice rather than the block plan. On the other hand, there was considerable concern about the student's lack of theoretical knowledge at the time he began working in the field. The study committee decided to limit the student's field placement to two days, rather than three, during his first semester at SASS. The study also developed a plan for offering students the opportunity to observe a broad range of social institutions throughout the city during the time allotted for the first five weeks of field placement. This plan, which would have broadened the student's knowledge of social welfare and would have delayed his entry into a specific social work agency, did not materialize. Instead, the School worked with the agencies to help them develop a more comprehensive student orientation program, which included information about social services that were used in conjunction with the operation of the particular agency.[20]

Considerable attention was devoted to ways in which the School might improve the quality of field instruction. Plans were made to develop a course in supervision for supervisors of staff in agencies in order to provide an experienced group of potential field instructors for future years. The School also planned to continue and expand its ongoing educational program for field instructors. The task of enabling the student to integrate his classroom and field learning had been a major function of the faculty adviser. The study recommended giving to the field instructor the key role in this process of integration. Faculty advisers continued to be assigned to field instructors in specific agencies to help expedite the School's educational program.[21]

The process of faculty advising was one of the most time-consuming of the faculty's duties. The study's examination of this program produced a number of changes in addition to the transfer of certain educational responsibilities to the School's field instructors. A committee on advising was established to develop policy on advising and to serve as a consultative body for both the dean and the faculty in relation to specific student problems. Recognizing that social work faculty tended to use casework techniques in contacts with students, the study recommended removing therapeutic and tutorial methods from the advising process.[22]

President Millis' concern about the operational expenses of SASS received careful attention during the 1952 study. The faculty instituted a time-study to determine how many hours it worked and how the time was apportioned. The time-study showed that an excessive amount of time was spent in community service, faculty advising, and committee work. On the other hand, far too little time was allotted to faculty research. An implicit objective of the self-study was to provide for better utilization of faculty time in relation to the total educational program of the School.[23]

The study recognized that the whole administrative process of the School was too complex and cumbersome. To some extent this was related to the fact that the School had had to adjust to the different modes of operation of three different deans over a relatively short period of time. Furthermore, the previous agency experience of many faculty members had produced a tendency "to adapt methods of social agency administration to the School, even though such methods [were] not always appropriate." On the other hand, the study committee believed that the particular function of a school of social work inevitably necessitated certain administrative programs and procedures not required in schools with regular academic programs. The field placement program required the establishment of special administrative relationships between the agencies and the School. The School handled grant-in-aid funds provided by the agencies and had to see that field practice was integrated with the educational experience in the classroom. A more involved admission procedure was required at SASS because of the need to secure students who were not only academically qualified but who also possessed personal maturity and the ability to work with people.[24]

After re-examining the internal organization of the School, the faculty decided to sweep away the complex committee structure that had grown up over the years in order to establish a more simplified system. Four standing committees were created: Administrative Policies, Classroom Program, Field Program, and Advising. They were to be supplemented by specialization committees in casework, group work, and community organization (when this specialization was fully developed). Generally, the specialization committees handled the more specific details of classroom and field teaching within their scope, as well as maintaining contact with related local and national organizations. The General Faculty Committee (all full-time faculty with the rank of assistant professor or higher) and The Faculty as Committee of the Whole (the entire faculty) remained a part of the School's organizational structure. The former was to make official faculty decisions, whereas the latter was to serve solely as a deliberative body. The new committee system provided for the rotation of committee membership and for monthly meetings, which were to be limited to two hours in duration when possible. To take over administrative functions which had formerly been handled by committees, the study recommended the appointment of an assistant dean and a full-time admissions officer.[25]

The study committee recommended a careful planning of faculty assignments based on a forty-hour week, which would provide time for research, community participation, and university participation as well as for activities more directly related to teaching. Although the faculty recognized that too large a proportion of its time had been spent in community activities, it strongly believed that such participation was of public relations value to the School and of professional value to the individual faculty member. The study committee recommended that faculty members consult with the dean before undertaking community responsibilities that would take time from their work week at the School, since in the past there had been some overlapping of faculty activity in the community.[26]

President Millis received the self-study report with enthusiasm even though he questioned some of the specific proposals, such as the advisory Committee on Administrative Policies—which he believed would usurp a function best performed by the dean. The president endorsed the recommendations for the new curriculum, but he considered the School's budget allocations too high for the number of students in SASS.[27]

Although subsequent financial limitations reduced the number of the faculty and prevented the immediate introduction of the proposed community organization program, the new curriculum was put into effect in the fall of 1954. The Council on Social Work Education invited the School to report on its new program at its annual meeting in January of 1955. The enthusiastic response was most satisfying to those who had worked untiringly on the self-study. So many social work educators were interested that the Council printed copies of the papers which had been presented by four members of the SASS faculty. Inquiries about the changed approach to social work education came from all over the United States and Canada, and four schools sent representatives to study the program at first hand. When the Russell Sage Foundation awarded a three-year grant to the School to conduct research on the application of the recent findings in the social sciences to the curriculum of a school of social work, Dr. Joseph Eaton came from Wayne University to direct the study and take part in the program of the School. The presence of a sociologist on the staff did much to stimulate thinking about the contributions of his field to social work.

The next few years saw a variety of changes and innovations. SASS co-operated with the medical school and the university's department of education in establishing a new program for nursery school preparation, and the School worked closely with other departments in the university to develop projects such as the Intergroup Relations Workshop and an Institute on the Care of the Aged and Chronically Ill in Philanthropic, Private and County Homes. The placement of an alumnus of SASS on the university's board of governors symbolized the more complete integration of the School with its parent body.

The financial situation of the School also began to show improvement after a few years. In addition to the established grants-in-aid from the city's social agencies, the Welfare Federation gave $30,000 over a period of three years to provide financial aid for students. Friends of the School gave money to furnish the new building and establish scholarships for students. A concerted effort to establish library facilities of high professional standards culminated in 1964 when SASS's library was dedicated to the memory of Margaret Allen Ireland, whose devotion to the School was of vital importance during the critical decade of the 1950's.

In 1955 the university permitted the School to engage in a two-million-dollar endowment drive. The Alumni Association responded by pledging a contribution of $50,000 and within a few years had exceeded this pledge by $17,000. The alumni response so impressed President Millis that he spurred the creation of a Citizens Committee to assist the School in the attainment of its goals. The new committee, under the leadership of W. C. Treuhaft, whose association with the School dated back to the early 1920's when he was on the advisory committee of the group service course, had raised over $250,000 by 1958.

The School and the Welfare Federation engaged in an active drive to recruit college students for careers in social work, and the expanded doctoral program began to attract able candidates. Gradually the faculty was restored to its former size. The National Institute of Mental Health's allocation of funds to SASS for the appointment of an associate professor was a harbinger of federal support, which was to strengthen the School's educational program in the future.

If the years immediately following the self-study gave new hope, they also provided moments of sadness. The 1950's saw the retirement of many faculty members who had creatively served their profession and their School during the early years: Agnes Schroeder, who had pioneered in the development of the School's medical social work; Anna Belle Tracy, whose services in the development of psychiatric social work were recognized by the creation of the Anna Belle Tracy Memorial Lecture Series in 1963; and Helen Walker, a member of the School's first training course in 1916, whose blithe spirit had sustained many students through the completion of their theses. In 1958 Margaret Johnson retired as dean. Under her leadership the School had met crisis with a searching analysis of its objectives and operations, and had emerged with a comprehensive program of social work education.

NOTES

1 Leonard W. Mayo to Walter Pettit, May 29, 1941.
2 Leonard W. Mayo to President W. G. Leutner, February 26, 1948.
3 Calvin Hall to Leonard W. Mayo, April 20, 1944.

4 "Annual Report of the School of Applied Social Sciences, 1943-1944," 15.

5 "A Report of the Study of the Program of the School of Applied Social Sciences of Western Reserve University: Conducted by the Faculty of the School in the Winter Session of 1952" (mimeographed, February, 1953), 3. Cited hereafter as "1952 Report."

6 Ernest V. Hollis and Alice L. Taylor, *Social Work Education in the United States* (New York: Columbia University Press, 1951), 215.

7 R. C. White, "Some Characteristics of S.A.S.S. Students. . ." (mimeographed, June, 1952).

8 "What the Alumni Think of SASS: With Some Interpretation of Its Meaning for Social Work Education at the School of Applied Social Sciences" (mimeographed, 1952), *passim*.

9 *Ibid*.

10 "1952 Report," 7.

11 *Ibid.*, 8-12.

12 Grace L. Coyle, "Objectives and Structure of the New Curriculum," *Developing an Integrated Curriculum: Curriculum Revision, School of Applied Social Sciences, Western Reserve University* (a pamphlet published by the Council on Social Work Education, 1955), 1-4. Cited hereafter as *Developing an Integrated Curriculum*.

13 "1952 Report," 17-19.

14 Raymond Fisher, "Growth and Development and Social Process," *Developing an Integrated Curriculum*, 8-10.

15 *Ibid.*, 10-12.

16 Virginia L. Tannar, "Social Welfare Organization and Practice," *Developing an Integrated Curriculum*, 12.

17 "1952 Report," 19, 21.

18 Virginia L. Tannar, "Social Welfare Organization and Practice," *Developing an Integrated Curriculum*, 16.

19 *Ibid.*, 16-19.

20 "1952 Report," 31-34, 36-37.

21 *Ibid.*, 37-38, 45.

22 *Ibid.*, 39-46.

23 "Report on the Time Study by the Ad Hoc Committee on Administration" (mimeographed, November 24, 1952).

24 "1952 Report," 55-56.

25 *Ibid.*, 63-74.

26 *Ibid.*, 75-76, 52.

27 President John S. Millis to Dean Margaret Johnson, September 8, 1953.

VI.   The Passing of the Torch

In 1958 Nathan E. Cohen was appointed the fifth dean of the School of Applied Social Sciences. Experienced in both administration and teaching, he came to SASS with a national reputation in the social work profession. After earning a Ph.D. degree in psychology from Harvard University, he had held executive positions with national social welfare organizations before he became associate dean of the New York School of Social Work in 1945. Cohen had also held important positions in national professional organizations, including the chairmanship of the National Committee on Social Work Education from 1949 to 1952. Just prior to his arrival at SASS he had published *Social Work in the American Tradition*, an examination of the evolution of the profession with an analysis of its strengths and its weaknesses. Some of the ideas he had expressed in the book—the importance of social workers' participating in social action, the need for more evaluative research, and the value of integrating new discoveries from the social sciences into social work curriculum—formed the framework for future program development at SASS.

Dean Cohen played an important part in moving the School in the direction that had been indicated by the 1952 study. As an able administrator within the School and an effective ambassador without, he gradually made the dean's office the locus of power for relating social work education to the needs of the community. His continuous dialogue with faculty members, agency representatives, and civic leaders stimulated new ideas and prepared the way for their implementation. His ability to secure increased financial support from local and national foundations and from the federal government enabled the School to improve old programs and engage in new ones.

In order to centralize the School's control over its educational program and at the same time to eliminate some of the administrative responsibility of the faculty, Dean Cohen gradually initiated several changes in the working relationship between SASS and its field placement agencies. By 1962 he was able to report that a number of the more progressive agencies had agreed to pool their grant-in-aid funds so that the School's admissions officer could undertake complete responsibility for allocating financial aid to qualified students. The change not only streamlined the School's admissions program but also relieved the faculty advisers of the need to handle this matter with individual agencies. On their part, those agencies that co-operated recognized that although they relinquished control of the funds (and the right to require a work commitment after graduation), they benefited in the long run from the fact that the School was in a better position to attract and select well-qualified students.

Another trend in the relationship between the School and field placement agencies was the increased use of student training-units for which the field instructors were full-time members of the SASS faculty. These units, which were financed primarily by grants from national organizations such as the National Institute of Mental Health, provided a larger number of field placements to meet the School's rising enrollment. While the students continued to be placed in traditional agency settings, the relationship between the class and field program was strengthened by the use of a faculty member as the field instructor.

The School's renewed effort to broaden and strengthen its program coincided with national concern about the internal problems of the United States. The rising tide of Negro protest against second-class citizenship threw new light on long-standing societal ills. The myth of pervasive American affluence gave way to the harsh reality of growing pockets of poverty. The technical proficiency revealed by the Russian sputnik shocked many Americans into a re-examination of their educational system. As the nation finally moved out of the complacency that had been the hallmark of the 1950's, the federal government and many private foundations turned to the universities to engage in research that would provide answers to society's problems.

The new dean of the School of Applied Social Sciences was already committed to a broad program of research and social action. He wrote:

Social work can best achieve its aims if it can help to shape the future course of social welfare events. To do so involves the development of leadership with the necessary knowledge, attitudes, and skills to administer large social welfare problems, evaluate existing policies, and to help in the creation of new policies and programs.[1]

To lay the groundwork for such a program the School, under Cohen's leadership, began to strengthen and expand its faculty and increase the size and quality of its student body.

The increased commitment by the university to the School was revealed by its willingness to undertake a larger share of its operating expenses and by the appointment of Mrs. Ralph S. Schmitt, the vice-president of the Board of Trustees, as the initial chairman of a permanent visiting committee for SASS. Mrs. Schmitt was succeeded by William C. Treuhaft. Under the imaginative leadership of its chairmen, the committee conducted several successful campaigns for increased endowment funds and did much to strengthen community support for the innovative changes that were taking place at the School.

Dean Cohen was anxious to organize a program of clinical and basic research to focus on (1) problems of social work theory and education, (2) problems of social work practice as they were faced by the agencies, and (3) social welfare questions of public policy and programs. Although the School had contemplated similar programs for a number of years, it was not until 1961 that a research center was established, with the help of a $50,000 grant from the Cleveland Foundation. A director was appointed to head the new center, which incorporated a number of ongoing faculty studies during its first year of operation. By 1963 the center had been involved in three major projects and several smaller ones; but it lost its director in 1962, and a year later Dean Cohen left SASS to become vice-president of the university. The original plan to establish well-financed interdisciplinary research was never achieved, and although the creation of an intra-university Center on Juvenile Delinquency was a partially successful outgrowth of the program, the research center went out of existence as a separate entity within the School. Nevertheless, the resulting focus on research was an important influence in strengthening the School's

educational program and also served to encourage and stimulate
research interest throughout the School.

During these years major advances were made in the advanced
educational program at SASS. These changes were given impetus
by the growing recognition among social work educators that the
time had come for the profession to increase education of its own
teachers and researchers. Furthermore, social work faculty members within a university setting who did not have the usual academic qualifications not only "lacked status" but also lagged in
attaining promotions and salary increases. As early as 1956 the
faculty of SASS had decided that in considering future appoint-
ments to its staff they would give preference to candidates with
advanced degrees.

In the 1950's there were two parts to the School's advanced program. A one-year course for experienced practitioners was "designed to deepen practice in case work, group work, or community organization, or to prepare for positions as supervisors or
consultants." The second part was the doctoral program, which
was planned to broaden the student's knowledge of social work,
deepen his knowledge of his own specialization, and encourage
him to make original contributions to the social work field. Doctoral candidates were expected to be "capable of giving a high
level of leadership, especially through teaching and research."
The curriculum included advanced courses in research; social
welfare policy, planning, and administration; and advanced seminars in a practice area; as well as social science courses from other
departments within the university. With the help of a grant from
the National Institute of Mental Health, the School was briefly
able to appoint an economist to its faculty to develop courses in
the economics of health and welfare and in comparative social
security systems. Considerable attention was given to determining
the best way in which to include behavioral science courses from
other parts of the university—whether the student should concentrate in one behavioral science or "take a light dip into several."
The increasing emphasis upon utilization of the contributions of
the behavioral scientists was further strengthened by the arrival
of Dean Herman D. Stein in 1964. Stein's collaboration with Rich-

ard A. Cloward had produced the first reader in the behavioral sciences for social work students.

By 1965 the Advanced Program Committee had decided to make a clear separation between the third-year program and the doctoral program, with the focus in the former to be the improvement of practice and in the latter to be scholarship and research. While a core set of courses for all doctoral students was established, the Committee decided to work out individual programs for each student in relation to one of the three career objectives of the doctoral program: (1) career researcher, (2) teacher of social-work method courses, (3) scholar or expert in administration and social policy. In 1965 the doctoral degree was changed from Doctor of Social Work, which had been granted by the graduate school of the university, to Doctor of Social Welfare, conferred as a professional degree by SASS.

In 1960 the School finally developed its first full program in community organization. In the 1940's and early 1950's Dean Leonard Mayo and Mildred Barry had pioneered in the development and establishment of a community organization sequence, but limited financial resources had prevented fuller development. Yet Cleveland, a city with a national reputation in the field of community welfare planning, offered excellent potential resources for field work. Under the leadership of John B. Turner attention was once more turned to this increasingly important area of social work. He established a master's program and later developed a doctoral program in community organization.

The focusing of attention on this aspect of social work reflected the desire of those within the School who wished to broaden the scope of their profession. They wanted to train their students to deal with the causes of social breakdown and to learn "how to deal with the power structure to bring about change." Dean Stein has written: "The emerging accents have been on 'community problem solving,' social action management, leadership development, community development, and the concept of community organization theory and practice is also increasingly oriented to analyzing the impact of basic economic forces on different strata of the population, and of examining and formulating social wel-

fare policies to provide services and programs for all as an endur-
ing part of the American social system."[2]

The national reputation of Dean Cohen and the growing recognition of the contributions of the community organization faculty
were in large part responsible for the Ford Foundation's decision
to ask SASS to take the leadership and responsibility for "Studies
of Priorities Determination in Community Planning." The School
accepted the task and the $460,000 grant that went with it. This
program permitted SASS to keep old faculty, add new members,
and provide a rich source of research material for advanced students. By 1963 the School was conducting research for the study
in five communities across the nation.

During the 1960's the faculty of SASS was once more reviewing
major areas of the master's curriculum. In part the need for curriculum re-examination was necessitated by the inclusion of new
material in community organization, but the experience of several
years with the new generic curriculum had also made the faculty
aware of shortcomings in the 1954 revision. In offering a strong
generic base, little provision had been made for electives that
would meet the needs of individual students. Additional course
offerings were also limited by the financial resources of the School.
As operating funds were expanded and the size of the faculty
increased, there was renewed interest in enlarging the academic
program.

A new study of the curriculum was also given impetus by a
qualitative change in the student body. The number of applicants
for admission to the School increased from 110 in 1958 to 198 in
1961. The increase made it possible for the School to be far more
selective in admitting students, and faculty members discovered
that many of their students came with a much better foundation
in the social sciences.

Curriculum revisions generally reflected faculty recognition of
the need to upgrade subject matter, achieve higher standards and
better integration of material, and avoid duplication with undergraduate courses. Earlier emphasis on the development of a common core of knowledge and the integration of material from the
social sciences and dynamic psychology remained important ob-

jectives. Similarly, the School continued to work on achieving "a balance between emphasis on the individual and the social institutions through which he functions and the public policy aspects of modern day society." On the other hand, there was new emphasis on providing a flexible educational program which would permit electives and movement into different levels of a given sequence depending on the background of the student.

There were major reorganizations in the sequences covering research, social welfare organization, growth and development, and psychopathology. It was the research sequence, which had received less attention in the 1952 study, that underwent the most basic change in terms of long-range objectives. In determining the central aim of research knowledge for the social work student, "it became clear [there was] an overall aim for all the students, but there were also more specific aims for . . . those students who had an interest and special ability in the areas of research and more abstract conceptualization." The faculty recognized that all students needed to have consumers' knowledge of research; course content would focus on how to understand and use research rather than how to do it. A smaller, selected group of students who were capable of dealing with higher levels of conceptualization and abstraction would be able to move ahead into courses dealing with the performance of basic research. All students would take an introductory course in social work research in the first semester. For the larger group of students a new sequence in applied research was added to the curriculum, whereas a more thorough sequence in basic research was planned for students who were qualified and interested in preparing for "future struggle with the theoretical issues of the field." The committee which studied the research sequence also re-examined the former practice of requiring all master's degree candidates to engage in group or individual research projects and decided that seminars geared to the needs and levels of the students would be more productive educationally. Under the new program both groups of students were given the opportunity to choose between taking a research seminar or engaging in a research project. The new research sequence was spread over a four-semester period and carried eight instead of six credits.

In July of 1964 Herman D. Stein became dean of the School of Applied Social Sciences, following Dean Cohen's appointment as vice-president of Western Reserve University. The new dean came to the School with impressive qualifications for directing a program of social work education. After graduating from the City College of New York in 1939, he was a Fellow in that school's Department of Government and Sociology for two years while he attended the New York School of Social Work at Columbia University. He received a master's degree in social work in 1941 and worked as a family caseworker for four years before he took the position of research instructor at the New York School of Social Work. Following World War II he served in Paris for three years as deputy director of the Welfare Department of the American Joint Distribution Committee. When he returned to the United States in 1950, he rejoined the faculty of the New York School of Social Work and began work toward a Doctorate in Social Welfare, which he was awarded in 1958. For the next six years he taught at the School and directed its Research Center. One of his major functions as research director was to organize and complete a significant faculty study of the New York School's curriculum. He held a number of important positions in various professional organizations and national and international governmental agencies. In addition, Stein's prolific writings on the need for increased applications of social science to social work practice made him one of the national leaders in curriculum policy development within the Council on Social Work Education.

Herman D. Stein was the first dean of the School of Applied Social Sciences to have risen through the ranks of the profession and the first to hold a D.S.W. from a school of social work. In many respects he represented the new maturity and scope of a profession whose horizons had broadened to encompass a worldwide perspective on the problems of social welfare. Following his overseas service during the postwar years he had become increasingly involved in international social work. His experience and knowledge relating to the needs of social workers in other parts of the world, particularly in the underdeveloped areas, gave new direction to the School's educational program for foreign students.

SASS had accepted foreign students since the 1920's, but there had never been more than a few enrolled at any one time. Before World War II little thought was given to the kind of education and practical experience that would be valuable to these students when they returned to face the problems of their native countries. While the School enjoyed a certain provincial pride in the presence of foreign students, a former dean of SASS commented in retrospect that there was a certain irrelevancy in giving courses in psychotherapy to prepare students for social welfare work in underdeveloped countries.

The involvement of the United States in the Second World War and in postwar reconstruction stimulated a renewed interest in attracting foreign students. Although the School became far less ethnocentric in its approach to providing social work education for students from other countries, there were still no broad policy formations to guide the faculty in the task of providing foreign students with an educational experience which would be useful to them when they returned home. The faculty advisers of these students spent an inordinate amount of time planning their educational programs and helping them with difficult problems of adjustment to a strange country. Despite the efforts of a few faculty members and students, the foreign nationals remained quite isolated from the student body.

In 1956 SASS began a program of co-operation with the Cleveland International Program for Youth Leaders and Social Workers (CIP). Of particular relevance to SASS was the fact that applicants from other countries which provided schools in social work and youth work were required to have completed their professional education and to have at least one or two years of working experience.[3] The CIP program played a part in focusing increased faculty attention on how the School could best meet the needs of foreign students, but it was not until Dean Stein arrived that the School revised its admission policy in relation to students from other countries. In an article written in 1963, the dean had articulated the premise underlying the change:

> While the profession of social work is international, and common
> elements are increasingly in evidence, it is not a technology or a

science requiring only minor adaptations to be universally appli-
cable wherever taught. Rather, it is still shaped in its ideology, by
the underlying social, economic, and cultural elements in each particular society in which it develops.[4]

The School's new admission policy for foreign students required
that they complete a school of social work in their own country
and have paid experience in the social welfare field in their country before being considered for the professional degree program
at SASS. The dean recognized that these requirements eliminated
foreign students who applied to the School immediately after completing an undergraduate college program in the United States.
While such students had an excellent knowledge of the language
and could easily adapt to the educational pattern, they were also
the students who were most likely to become alienated from conditions in their own countries. They were frequently unable to
use the professional course of study in the United States in relation to social welfare needs and real conditions at home.

Another area to which the new dean turned his attention was
the administrative problems of the School. In 1917 when SASS
completed its first year of operation, its total budget was nine
thousand dollars, two-thirds of which was allocated to the public
health nursing program. There were few full-time faculty members, and there was only one agency for training students. As SASS
moved into its fiftieth year of operation, the budget had passed
the one million dollar mark; there were forty-seven full-time faculty members; and the number of field placements had increased
to forty-seven.

Much of the expansion occurred after 1958 and was not accompanied by any systematic revision of the School's administrative
structure. In fact, the failure to do so during Cohen's stewardship
reflected his approach toward running the school. One faculty
member recalled that Cohen liked a free-wheeling atmosphere.
He was much like Franklin D. Roosevelt in his creativeness and
pragmatism; "starting things without tying up all the ends, seem-
ing to enjoy watching faculty subgroups battle it out at faculty
meetings." The School was going through a period of transition.
Established ideas about approaches to social work education were

being challenged by innovative faculty members, and one of the results for the school was creative turmoil, but turmoil nonetheless. In such a transitional period a rigid pattern of administration, where roles and responsibility were clearly spelled out, might well have foreclosed discussion and change.

As the academic dust began to settle, it became increasingly clear that the expansion of the faculty and the student body and the enlargement of the School's role in the community necessitated a different approach. This need was met by Dean Stein when he arrived in 1964. He took a close look at the existing administrative structure and its effect upon the educational role of the school and then reorganized the Office of Admissions and the Registrar's Office in order to simplify procedure and clarify lines of responsibility. Administrators were relieved of many duties that could be handled by clerical personnel.

A major innovation was the establishment of a Department of Field Work. In 1965 Dean Stein reported:

> In the increasingly complex activities of a professional school such as ours, the absence of a central source for management of the field work enterprise creates serious weaknesses. Chief among these weaknesses is serious unevenness—in standards applied to agencies of field instruction, in maintaining systematic reporting of field instruction by agency personnel, in field adviser's responsibilities, and particularly in lack of coordination and administrative supervision of the faculty field instructors themselves.[5]

Within the new department the former responsibilities of the case-work, group work, and community organization committees remained intact, but the overall administrative responsibilities for field placements were assigned to a director of field work and admissions, who was to head the department. The new director, who received administrative reports from all faculty field instructors (in training units), was responsible for periodic review of the educational standards of field placements, and for exploring new potential resources for field instruction.

The School's increased use of full-time field instructors led to a serious consideration of their position in relation to the rest of the faculty. While many of these field instructors were not interested in working for an advanced degree, the faculty took the position they should consider themselves primarily as educators rather than practitioners. Insofar as they engaged in general academic activities such as study, teaching, research, and writing, they should be eligible for recognition in rank and salary. They should not be regarded, in the Orwellian sense, as "less equal" because they did not possess D.S.W. degrees. Eventually the School hoped to have a unified faculty in which there would be no status distinction between class and field teachers. In 1966 the School moved in this direction when several of the full-time field instructors were promoted to assistant professors in recognition of their contributions to the education and training of students. On the other hand, there would be no change in the position of agency field instructors, who were primarily responsible to their agencies.

In 1964 the School had to review its entire educational program in preparation for accreditation by the Council on Social Work Education, which had recently adopted a policy requiring periodic reports on schools and departments of social work. That the tasks of review and writing reports placed a heavy burden on the faculty is evidenced by the three weighty volumes that were produced during the study. The close examination of the School's curriculum encouraged the dean and the faculty to organize a Curriculum Committee to centralize responsibility for ongoing review. The Committee was expected to keep abreast of new subject matter as well as to maintain an integrated and balanced curriculum.

During the 1960's the School's evaluation of its educational program in relation to broad needs in the field of social welfare resulted in a serious dialogue concerning the manpower shortage in social work. The faculty approached the problem with much greater professional security than it had felt in relation to the influx of "aides" during the Depression. Not only were faculty members willing to assist agencies in organizing in-service training programs for personnel who did not have professional education, but they also began to consider how people with far less education than the professional social worker could be utilized in providing welfare services. Implicit in this thinking was the possibility of "some re-definition of the role and function of the professional worker."

This concern about the "role and function" of the social worker was accentuated by the growing civil rights movement and the ensuing war on poverty. Like the social work profession, SASS throughout its history has had a better than average record in providing education and opportunities for Negro students. Faculty members such as Grace Coyle were devoted to securing justice for Negro citizens, but placement of students was for some time governed by the wishes of the agencies.

In 1963 Cleveland's complacency was shattered by the rising discontent of the Negro community over inadequate school facilities. Dean Cohen called the faculty together to examine the role of the School in this and other civil rights questions. He gained complete support from the faculty when he declared that the School should no longer tolerate any hidden discrimination in the placement of students. Agencies that engaged in such discrimination could no longer count upon the School's acquiescence in such practices. Indeed, many of the faculty members were already active leaders in attempts to end discriminatory practices at both local and national levels.

During the 1930's, when students and graduates were raising questions about the need for courses in social action, someone had wondered about field experience on a picket line. Thirty years later many of the faculty members and students had spent enough time on picket lines protesting racial discrimination to have "earned" many credit hours. It became increasingly clear that for the faculty and the students of SASS the older approach of adjusting the individual to his society was being replaced by one that considered the possibility of readjusting society to the needs of individuals.

Nowhere was this changing approach to social work more evident than in the faculty's concern about a successful conclusion to the national drive for victory over poverty. When this "war" was started in 1964, SASS faculty members were among the leaders on the local battlefields. They provided new strategies in the fight against poverty and brought their professional knowledge and expertise to break down traditional responses to this question. A good example of the School's new role was Dean Stein's keynote address to a 1965 NASW institute on "The Impact of the Poverty Program in Cleveland upon Social Work Practice and Knowledge." Stein declared that "In public welfare we tacitly comply with a punitive and demeaning approach to people and grossly disregard, in the law, in administrative policy and in daily practice the most important qualities in caring for the needs and the human dignity of the poor." He called upon social workers not to "passively accept miserable and inhuman conditions in our public agencies" and to "serve as the conscience of society in behalf of the deprived."[6]

These words were followed by action in early 1966 when the Cleveland Protestant Ministry to Poverty presented a $250,000 proposal to the Council for Economic Opportunities in Greater Cleveland. Under the proposal the poor of the eastern Hough area of Cleveland were to be organized to help themselves through political action. There was considerable opposition by some established welfare agencies and political leaders, but the plan did win support from many agency executives. When the matter was debated before the Economic Opportunities Council, Dean Stein called for endorsement of the proposed plan. He acknowledged that there were risks involved but declared that the central idea of the project was to make it possible for people who feel powerless to act on their own behalf. While there were some aspects of the proposals on which he had reservations, he viewed favorable action "as an act of civic courage, representing confidence in its citizens . . . and new light for the nation's cities on the merits and weaknesses of attempts to organize the poor under the auspices of local and national government."[7]

Questions of how social work education can best meet its societal responsibilities reflect the essence of the intellectual ferment that afflicts the profession today. The new generation of social workers has moved from a preoccupation with the ills of the individual to a broader concern which encompasses the maladjustments of a society which is in a state of massive flux. As early as 1951 the Hollis-Taylor report recognized that:

The profession has accepted too little of a unified responsibility for appraising and improving social welfare institutions. A continuation of the concern with improving the direct rendering of service to individuals and groups to the neglect of a study of the causes of individual and social maladjustment and the possibilities of broader programs of prevention, will seriously limit the expanding role of social work.[8]

Fourteen years later the new dean of SASS re-emphasized the importance of including a "strong social policy orientation" in social work education:

The student should be helped to project his experience beyond the confines of his own work and even that of the agency itself; helped to raise questions, in other words, about the meaning of the problems facing the agency's clientele, the significance of the agency's efforts to solve them, in order to consider further what more might be done through legislation or other broader approaches.[9]

Why has it taken social work so long to come to terms with the environmental causes of individual incapacity? Grace Coyle once noted that "social work has always been dominated by two factors: the social climate in which it moves and the state of the sciences on which it is dependent."[10] When the movement for a school of social work was first initiated in Cleveland, the social climate was geared to change. It was a cruel irony of fate that SASS finally came into existence when the progressive era was in its ebb tide. It was not the social reform of the settlement house movement, but the moralism of the charity organization movement that was the lingering heritage of the School of Applied Social Sciences. The Associated Charities, which dominated the School during its formative years, was supported by a society that had reverted to the individualism of earlier years. The consequent emphasis on adjusting the individual to the society was reinforced by the profession's hasty incorporation of psychiatric theory. When the Depression abruptly shattered the optimism of the 1920's, Americans were once again ready to accept social reform; but social workers were operating on such a narrow scientific base that they were not equipped to give leadership to the new social welfare programs. By 1938 the School was in the process of a serious examination of its role in relation to the emerging field of public welfare, but the outbreak of World War II diverted the nation's attention away from domestic problems.

As social workers mastered the skills of therapeutic intervention, they became increasingly secure in their professional identity and began to evaluate the social work process. During the postwar period it was study and research, rather than a progressive commitment to social reform, that put the "social" back in "social work." By the 1960's when the society again turned its attention to the burgeoning problems of social welfare, the profession was ready: its base of knowledge had expanded to encompass the rapid growth of the social sciences; its method had been developed to include intervention in the community process, as well as individual and group processes; and the foundation had been laid for significant scientific inquiry within the profession. The School of Applied Social Sciences was ready to live up to its name.

NOTES

[1] Cohen, 352.

[2] Herman D. Stein, "Observations on Determinants of Social Work Education in the United States" (a paper delivered at the Intercultural Seminar, East-West Center, Hawaii, February 21–March 4, 1966), 24.

[3] Henry B. Ollendorff, "CIP—A Jointly Sponsored Program for Foreign Visitors," International Educational and Cultural Exchange, Fall, 1965 (U. S. Advisory Commission on International Educational and Cultural Affairs, U. S. Government Printing Office, 1965), 46-55.

[4] Quoted in Stein, "Observations on Determinants of Social Work Education in the United States," 1.

[5] Dean Herman D. Stein, "Annual Report to the President of Western Reserve University on the School of Applied Social Sciences: 1964-65," 15.

[6] The Cleveland Press, October 9, 1965.

[7] Herman D. Stein, "Statement at Public Hearing on December 29, of Proposal Review Subcommittee of Council for Economic Opportunities to Review the 'Eastern Hough Organized for Action' Demonstration Proposal."

[8] Hollis and Taylor, 142.

[9] Herman D. Stein, "Cross-Currents in Practice, Undergraduate, and Graduate Education in Social Work" (a paper delivered to the Council on Social Work Education, 13th Annual Program Meeting, January 19-21, 1965), 14.

[10] Grace L. Coyle, "Social Work at the Turn of the Decade," Proceedings of the National Conference of Social Work, 1940, 12.

Epilogue

The Fiftieth Anniversary of the School of Applied Social Sciences of Western Reserve University was celebrated the last week of September, 1966, by means of an exciting colloquium of scholars. For each of the four major sessions of the colloquium, there was an attendance of over one thousand, including deans and professors of schools of social work throughout the United States and Canada; academicians from many fields in the metropolitan Cleveland university community; distinguished representatives from business, politics, and the professions; alumni of the School; students; and citizens from all walks of life.

It was a brilliant occasion in the history of the School, marking not so much the attainment of a golden anniversary, as the new vistas which are now open to the School and to the social work profession. The theme of the colloquium was Social Theory and Social Invention—The Translation of Ideas and Knowledge into Action for the Welfare of Society.

By means of this theme the School was in a sense reaffirming and recasting in today's terms the hope of the School's founders, who wished to organize a professional school wherein the social sciences would be drawn upon for direct application to the needs of society and community affairs. The colloquium was in part a challenge to the social sciences to see how theory has been and could be capitalized upon for social invention, just as in the biological and physical sciences theory has led to bold inventive applications. It signified as well the great opportunity and challenge to social work to expand the scope of its usefulness to society by broadening the range of its concerns and deepening its base of scientific knowledge for wider and increasingly more significant application.

The celebration opened with an impressive academic convocation of scholars, who heard an address by the Honorable Abba Eban, Minister of Foreign Affairs from Israel. The major papers presented at the colloquium were by the renowned social economist, Gunnar Myrdal, of Sweden; the Honorable Charles Frankel, philosopher and Assistant Secretary of State for Education and Cultural Affairs; Michael Harrington, author of *The Other America*; and Melvin M. Tumin, sociologist, of Princeton University. The discussants included Eugen Pusic of Yugoslavia, Dame Eileen L. Younghusband of England, Lucien Mehl of France, and from the United States Professors Eveline M. Burns and Richard A. Cloward of Columbia University, Alton A. Linford and George F. Rohrlich of the University of Chicago, Charles I. Schottland of Brandeis University, Irving Rosow and John B. Turner of Western Reserve University, Julia Henderson, Director of the United Nations Bureau of Social Affairs, Whitney M. Young, Jr., Executive Director of the National Urban League, and Ellen Winston, United States Commissioner of Welfare.

The papers and discussions were hard hitting, realistic, and incisive. There were sharp differences of views about the extent to which social theory has contributed to social invention and the conditions under which it could contribute. There was no disagreement, however, about the vital necessity of such a contribution, nor about its being mandatory that schools such as the School of Applied Social Sciences become increasingly involved in helping shape the course of human affairs.

The theme selected by the School to signal the transition into its future; the broad range of backgrounds of those invited to participate; and the enthusiastic reception of the academic, professional, and lay communities to both focus and speakers all served to underline the mandate to which the School has increasingly become committed: to define the most significant human problems with which the profession of social work can usefully be concerned; to direct and utilize the School's resources of knowledge, research, and practice to contribute to the solution of those problems by harnessing its efforts to those of related sciences and professions; and to venture more directly into the arena of public policy on the basis of knowledge and competence.

—Herman D. Stein

Index